Party Party

Party Party

Nirmala Tilak

Popular Prakashan
Mumbai

Popular Prakashan Pvt. Ltd.
35-C, Pt. Madan Mohan Malviya Marg
Popular Press Bldg., Tardeo
Mumbai - 400 034

First Published 2000

(3596)

ISBN-81-7154-554-8

PRINTED IN INDIA
By Tarun Enterprises, Delhi
and Published by Ramdas Bhatkal for
Popular Prakashan Pvt. Ltd., 35-C
Pandit Madan Malaviya Marg.
Tardeo, Mumbai - 400 034

Acknowledgements

I owe a lot to my husband and children for their constant support and love. It was their inspiration and encouragement that gave me the enthusiasm to experiment with different food-stuffs and most of all to write this book. I also would like to thank my daughter Shaila Nene and daughter-in-law Aparna Tilak for their help in the translation.

Introduction

It is a huge problem! What does one cook for these vegetarian guests? It is always difficult to cook for vegetarian guests, especially when the hosts of the party are non-vegetarians themselves. Similarly on holidays and on Sundays what special dishes does one prepare to please everyone in the house? What quick snacks can one cook for the kids when they come from school?

This book will definitely provide some answers to these dilemmas of everyday cooking.

There are a wide variety of cookbooks available in the Marathi language for beginners. This has been a great help to girls with keen interest in cooking. The main aim of this book is meant to tackle the problem: how to cook? It basically will be more appealing to those women who have some knowledge about basic cooking or for those who have the interest in experimenting with new food stuffs and novel ideas to make vegetarian food more popular and appealing to the palate. When one invites guests over, the big question is - what should be the menu? This book presents the reader with certain menus consisting of an ensemble of different food stuffs and thus makes it easier to take quick decisions.

Majority of the people go to hotels to savour delicious meals. On some occasions one gets tired of the daily routine or certain dishes cannot be cooked at home so one goes to restaurants for a change. But I am certain that the recipes in the book, if followed accurately will make dishes that will not only be comparable to hotel food but may be even better. And all this at less than half the cost. Moreover the food prepared outside may be contaminated as the oil, the cleanliness or the places where they are prepared may not be up to the standards one has at home.

While compiling this book together, I have kept one view point in mind. I have not only written recipes that will cater to Maharashtrian tastes but have included cullinary delights from other regions as well as international all-time favourites. In today's fast changing cosmopolitan world it is very important to keep an open mind to the never and ever changing tastes of people.

While trying out some particular recipe, it is quite possible that one of the ingredients may not be available easily or you might not have it at home at that time. Do not panic. There are alternatives which can be used in their place. The translations of certain words are provided in Hindi and English for your ease. Another important thing is, why does a particular dish fail? It is extremely important to understand the reasons for this. If one is aware of this, then one takes all the precautions to avoid a culinary disaster. The reason why a dish fails and how to prevent it is also presented in this book.

To save time certain steps of a dish can be prepared the previous day or sometime before starting to prepare the dish. Certain Maharashtrian sweet delicacies like 'Jalebi', 'Shrikhand', 'Basundi' are so filling and delicious that very often it is noticed that the guests cannot do justice to the other dishes on the table. Normally after dinner the guests are always in a hurry to leave. Therefore the foreign concept of 'desserts' is a very good way to make your guests taste something sweet after their meal, which is not very rich and at the same time enjoyable. This idea is fast gaining popularity as it makes it easier for the host to plan a good meal along with something sweet to end it. You will find a variety of desserts in this book.

After reading this book thoroughly, it will become explicitly clear that this book will be a great help to you in preparing special dishes for special occasions. It will also prove beneficial in many other respects. Amateur cooks can prepare most of the dishes after a little practice. The most important thing is that one should be prepared to work hard and have a keen interest to learn. Once a person is ready to do this then nothing is impossible.

I have personally tried these recipes often before putting them on paper. The different weights and measures mentioned in this book are easily available in the market place. If you use them systematically then all your dishes are bound to be perfect.

In this book I have given the reader an arbitrary idea of how many people a particular dish will cater to. This is only an approximate figure. Each individual's likes, dislikes, capacity to eat, etc. can change this arbitrary figure. Similarly a certain dish, even if prepared in a lesser quantity might be enough when there is a variety of other delicacies but if only that one dish is prepared then one has to increase the quantity accordingly. But this decision is yours solely.

To become an expert in the 'Art of Cooking' is not very difficult. With the help of good information, guidance, interest and direction, any person can cook great, tasty and wholesome meals. There are certain tips that I would like to share with you :

(i) Weights, measures, oven temperature, ingredients, reasons why a dish does not turn out well, solutions to it, should be read with care.
(ii) Read the beginning of each chapter carefully.
(iii) Before starting any recipe read each one line by line so as not to miss any important detail.
(iv) Before actually starting the cooking process keep the equipment and ingredients required ready.
(v) Weigh and measure each ingredient carefully. This may be time consuming but in the long run it is much better than facing a dish that is completely ruined.
(vi) Understand the recipe properly before starting. Those ingredients that can be made ready in advance should be prepared to save time.
(vii) Things used for decoration should be exclusively used for that purpose only. Those decorations which are not edible should be avoided. Give more importance to the tastiness of the whole dish.
(viii) The quantity of salt, chilli powder should be varied in accordance to the taste, likes and dislikes of the people you are cooking for.

Although women may excel and progress in many other spheres of life, this sphere which is ours exclusively, which is the essence of womanhood, should not be neglected. After all it is the woman who is called the 'Ghar ki Rani'. They say that the way to a man's heart is through his stomach. You can cook a lot of tasty and mouth-watering dishes and win the hearts of everyone at home. Along with the admiration of those who you invite you will find them licking their fingers and asking for more.

Nirmala Tilak

Weights and Measures

The weights and measures used to prepare the dishes in this book are in the spoon and cup form. These are easily available in the market.

Water or Liquid Ingredients

1 tea spoon - 5 m.l
1 dessert spoon - 8 m.l (1 ½ tsp.)
1 table spoon - 15 m.l (3 tsp.)
1 ounce - 30 m.l
1 cup - 8 ounces (liquid water)
1 pint - 16 ounces
1 gill - 5 ounces

Metric

1 ounce - 28 to 30 grams
4 ounces - 112 to 115 grams
16 ounces - 450 to 454 grams - 1 pound
500 grams - ½ kilo
1000 grams - 1 kilo

Maida - 2 tbsp. full - 1 ounce - ¼ cup (level)
4 ounces - 1 cup (level)
Castor Sugar - 2 tbsp. full - 2 ounces - ¼ cup
Sugar - 3 tbsp. full - 2 ounces - ¼ cup full
Brown Sugar - 1 tbsp. full - 1 ounce - 30 grams
Butter or Margarine (melted) - 2 tbsp. (level) - 1 ounce
1 cup (level) - 8 ounces
Cornflour - 2 tbsp. full - 1 ounce
Jam - 1 tbsp. - 1 ounce
Cocoa - 2 tbsp. full - 1 ounce
Self Raising Flour - For 1 cup (115 grams)
add 1 tsp. baking powder

Preparation Techniques

Some Important Methods

Serial No. 1 :- Masalas used for cooking

Basically all the masalas are available in the market. But we can never be sure of the quality. Sometimes the date of manufacture is not mentioned either. While preparing cumin seed powder and whole coriander powder in large quantities they are given over to flour-mills to grind. While they are being ground there, the heat of the machines is so great, that they can get burnt, which diminishes their flavour and taste. Therefore it is better and easy to prepare the above mentioned powders of masalas at home, with the help of modern amenities like the mixer. The powders and spices prepared at home enhance the taste of a dish and we are sure of the quality of the masalas.

Goda Masala : Whole coriander - ¼ kilo, White sesame seeds - 100 grams, Cloves - 15 grams, Badiyaam (star anise) - 10 grams, Nagkeshar - 10 grams, Bay leaves - 10 grams, Dagad phool - 10 grams, Cumin seeds - 15 grams, Black cumin seeds - 10 grams, Red chillies - 25 grams, Cinnamon - 15 grams, Turmeric (full) - 3 (root form), Asafeotida - beetlenut size.

All the above mentioned ingredients should be roasted well and separately in little oil. The sesame seeds should be roasted without oil. All the above ingredients should be pounded or ground in a mixer to make a fine powder. Sieve and add a little salt. Keep this in an air-tight container. This masala is more often used in the Brahmani style of cooking.

Saraswat Masala : Red chillies - ¼ kilo, Whole coriander - 100 grams, 1 heaped tbsp. Black cumin, 1 heaped tbsp, Black pepper, 1 tbsp. Cloves, cinnamon - 10 grams, 6 Bay leaves, Black cardamom - 12 pieces, Poppy seeds -100 grams, Nutmeg - 2 whole, 4 Turmeric roots - handful Dagad phool, Nagkeshar - 1 tbsp, Badiyaam (star anise) - 10 grams, Fennel seeds - 1 tsp.

The above ingredients (except black cumin and poppy seeds) should be roasted well in little oil. Cumin seeds, poppy seeds and black cumin seeds should be lightly roasted separately without oil. After grinding to a fine powder, store in an air-tight bottle. This masala is often used to prepare chicken and mutton dishes. If this masala is used in certain vegetarian sprouts recipes, curries or dals, a very different and novel taste can be achieved

Sambhar Masala : Red chillies - 10, Whole coriander - 50 grams, Black pepper - 20, Fenugreek seeds - 1 tbsp., Gram dal - 1 tbsp., Split black beans - ½ tbsp.

All the above mentioned ingredients should be roasted without oil. Pound the above and make a fine powder. Store in an air-tight bottle. It is due to this masala that the Madrasi Sambhar gets its delicious taste.

Rasam Masala : Whole coriander - 50 grams, Red chillies - 8 to 10, Fenugreek seeds - 1 tsp., Cumin seeds - 1 tsp., Black pepper - 15 to 20, Mustard - ½ tsp., Turmeric roots - 1, Asafoetida - ¼ tsp.

Roast the above ingredients well on a low flame. Pound it and make a fine powder. Store in an air-tight bottle.

Garam Masala : Cumin seeds - 20 grams, Black pepper - 10 grams, Cinnamon - 10 grams, Cloves - 10 grams, Black cardamom - 10 grams

Do not roast the above ingredients. Just pound it. The black cardamom should be pounded along with its skin. Store this powder in an air-tight bottle. This masala is used in Punjab and Uttar Pradesh.

Kashmiri Garam Masala : Black cardamom- 20 pieces, Black cumin seeds - 1 tbsp., Black pepper - 1 tbsp., Cloves - 1 tbsp. Cinnamon - 7 grams, Mace - 3 leaves, Nutmeg - ¼ tbsp.

The above ingredients should be pounded raw to a fine powder. Sieve and store in an air-tight jar. It is better to prepare small quantities of cumin seed powder and whole coriander powder and cinnamon powder as they are used frequently (about 50 grams at a time - as freshness lasts for 15 days). Masalas and powder should be prepared in small amounts. If they are made in large quantities, they tend to lose their aroma and flavour. If such masalas are used in cooking, then the food does not turn out as delicious as it should.

Chat Masala : Rock salt - 30 grams, Black pepper - 20 grams, Dry ginger - 10 grams, Cumin seeds - 10 grams, Black cumin seeds - 5 grams, Bay leaves - 3, Citric granules - 6 grams, Black cardamom - 6, Green cardamoms, 4, Pinch of Asafoetida, Nutmeg - 1 small, Mace - 4 grams, Cinnamon - 5 grams, Cloves - 5 grams

Pound citric acid granules and rock salt separately. Pound the remaining ingredients fine. The pounded citric acid granules and the rock salt should be mixed with the other pounded masala. Sieve through a flour sieve and keep in an air-tight container.

Green chillies, garlic and ginger for everyday use should be ground separately to a fine paste and kept in containers in the fridge.

Serial No. 2 :- The Double Boiler Process

Take two vessels that fit loosely into each other. That is lower half of the top vessel should sit at a height of half the height of the lower one. In other words the bottom of the top utensil should not be in contact with the water in the lower one. The amount of water to be put in the lower utensil should be so much that the bottom part of the top utensil should not touch it. First boil the water in the lower utensil. Then remove it from the gas. Place the other utensil in it and add the ingredients as mentioned in the recipe and beat the mixture till it turns light and custard like. Remove the top utensil and beat the mixture for a little while. The mixture prepared by this method does not tend to curdle.

Serial No. 3 :- Tomato Puree

To boiling water add tomatoes. Give two boils and remove from fire. After it cools slightly, the tomatoes should be taken out from the water and peeled. Put the tomatoes in the mixer and make the puree. Strain this through a strainer, continuously pressing it with a wooden spoon.

Serial No. 4 :- Caramel

Preparation Time - 5 minutes **Cooking Time - 5 minutes**

Ingredients

Sugar : 3 heaped tbsp.
or 10 to 15 sugar cubes
water : 2 tbsp.
Lemon Juice or Vinegar (white) :
¼ tsp.

Method

i) Take a small utensil with a thick bottom. Do not use a stainless steel vessel. Use a brass one. To this add sugar, water and lemon juice and place it on the gas. When the water begins to boil and the colour changes, move the vessel slightly and stir till it reaches the desired colour and remove from fire. For coating the mould pour quickly into the mould such that it coats the inner sides and the bottom of the mould well.

ii) If you wish to add caramel to milk, then when the caramel is ready, add two tbsp. of water. After it melts add it to the milk.

Serial No. 5 :- White Sauce (thick)

Preparation Time : 5 minutes **Cooking Time - 10 minutes** **Makes 1 Cup**

Ingredients

Flour : 2 tbsp.
Butter (soft and level) : 1 tbsp.
Salt : ¼ tsp.
Pepper : ¼ tsp.
(if mentioned in the recipe)
Milk : 1 cup

Method

i) Melt the butter in a vessel and add the flour to it. Stir till they both blend together. The colour should not be allowed to change.

ii) Add little quantities of hot milk to it while stirring continuously. Use a good wooden spoon for stirring. Do not allow lumps to be formed. After the entire milk is added don't let it boil for too long. Remove from the gas and add salt. If you wish to or like the taste or if written in the recipe, then add pepper and mix together. This sauce can be used for baked vegetables or augratins.

White sauce (thin)

Flour : 1 tbsp.
Butter : 1 tbsp.
Salt : ¼ tsp.
Milk : ½ cup
Pepper : ¼ tsp.
(if mentioned in the recipe)

Process

i) Proceed in the same way as mentioned above.

ii) This sauce is used in soups and to coat boiled vegetables.

In the thick white sauce ½ cup grated cheese can be added. Then it becomes a cheese sauce. If ½ tsp. mustard powder is added, then it becomes a mustard sauce. Prepare the white sauce in quantities mentioned above.

Serial No. 6 :- Breadcrumbs

Ingredients

Plain Jeera Butter Biscuits : 100 grams (available in markets)

Method

i) Pound butter biscuits to a coarse powder. You can do this in a dry grinder. These can be used as "breadcrumbs".

Important Note : *If butter biscuits are not easily available then you should toast bread to a brown colour and crush it.*

Serial No. 7 :- Paneer

Ingredients

Milk : 1 litre
Lemon Juice : 2 to 3 tsp.
A Pinch of Salt

Method

i) Put the milk to boil.
ii) When it begins to boil add salt and lemon juice. The milk will immediately start to curdle.
iii) When the water and the residue begins to separate, turn off the gas.
iv) The curdled part should be placed in a muslin cloth and tied. After the water drains out place a weight on this so that the remaining water also is removed. This will make 200 grams of paneer.

Important Note : *Do not use milk which is already boiled and the malai removed.*

Serial No. 8 :- Curd Cheese

Ingredients

Milk : ½ litre
Curds : 2 tsp.

Method

i) Warm the milk.
ii) Beat curds and add to the lukewarm milk. Stir well. Cover and keep aside.
iii) After the curds are formed, place in a muslin cloth. Tie them light to allow the whey to drip.
iv) When the curd feels dry, the curd cheese is ready to use.

Serial No. 9 :- Chillies in Vinegar

Ingredients

Green Chillies : 4 to 6
White Vinegar : 2 tbsp.
Salt : ½ tsp.
Sugar : ½ tsp.

Method

i) Cut chillies to fine slices - 1/8 inch wide.
ii) In a wide mouthed bottle put the chillies and the other ingredients and place the cover on it and shake it well.
iii) Use it after 2 days.

• • •

Contents

• • •

Indian Breads

Even today it is a very common practice not to eat bread or serve it on the table along with our meals. It somehow doesn't feel right. Rotis, phulke, puris are hot favourites on the dining table. These days parathas, naan and kulchas are also commonly prepared. That's why it is important to have the knowledge about some dos and don'ts while preparing them.

(i) While preparing the dough, oil or ghee should be rubbed into the flour well and then it should be kneaded properly. Before making puris or rotis, the dough should be kneaded at least one hour in advance.

(ii) While making puris, a pinch of sugar can be added to the dough. The ready dough should be on the harder side. The use of flour should be restricted as far as possible or not used at all while rolling out the puris.

(iii) Sometimes if the dough lacks stickiness then add a spoonful of flour (maida) and knead.

(iv) While preparing layered (folded) rotis or parathas, first divide the dough into balls, roll each in a round shape like a puri. Now apply ghee or oil and sprinkle rice flour. Or mix ghee and rice flour to a paste and apply on it. Then fold in half. Apply oil, ghee or paste and fold again to a quarter. Now start to roll it. Roast on a gridle. While roasting parathas, put ghee on the gridle first.

Naan

Preparation Time - 15 minutes **Cooking Time - 30 minutes** **12 to 14 Naans**

Ingredients

Flour (maida) : 2 cups (460 gms)
Baking Powder : 1 tsp.
Ghee (method) : 3 tbsp.
Curds : 4 to 5 tbsp.
Kallonji : 1 tbsp.
Salt to taste

Equipments

A curve bottomed gridle with a handle or a gas tandoor

Method

(i) Sieve the flour, baking powder and salt together.
(ii) Add curds and water to the flour mixture and knead to a soft dough.
(iii) Keep the dough in a warm place covered with a wet cloth for 8 to 10 hours.
(iv) After 2 hours add ghee (melted), knead well, cover and keep aside.
(v) Roll the naan in a long shape (thickish). Apply water on one side. When the gridle is hot place naan, with the wet side down. Sprinkle 10 to 12 kallonji seeds on top. Once it puffs, turn the gridle upside down on the gas.
(vi) When the naan is ready, smear it with ghee or butter. Serve hot.

Important Note : *The gridle to be used should be scrubbed and washed well with hot water at least three or four times. The gridle should not be sticky or oily.*

Palak Puri

Preparation Time - 15 minutes **Cooking Time - 20 minutes** **75 Puris**

Ingredients

Palak : 1 bunch
Wheat : 2 to 2 ½ cups
Oil : 2 to 3 tbsp.
Salt to taste

Masala for Grinding

Garlic Cloves : 8
Ginger : ½ inch
Green Chillies : 4
Oil to fry

Method

(i) Remove the stalks from the palak. Clean and wash well. Grind to a fine paste.
(ii) Add oil, salt, ground masala, wheat flour and knead to consistency. Do not add water (Add enough flour to get a hard, not soft ball consistency).
(iii) Roll out the puris and fry them in oil.
(iv) Serve hot with chhunda.

Batata Puri

Preparation Time - 15 minutes **Cooking Time - 15 minutes** **15 to 20 Puris**

Ingredients

Flour : 1 cup
Medium Sized Potatoes : 2
Lemon Juice : 2 to 3 tsp.
Oil : 2 tsp. (mohan)
Salt to taste
Oil for frying

Method

(i) Boil the potatoes.
(ii) While they are still hot, peel and mash them, add lemon juice and mix well.
(iii) Add the oil to the flour and rub it in well.
(iv) The potato mixture and flour should be kneaded well, ½ an hour before making the puris.
(v) Before frying puris add salt and knead well.
(vi) Roll out puris and fry till golden brown.

***Important Note :** Puris should be served hot. That's when they taste the best. These taste great with chole (recipe given in the book).*

Bhature

Preparation Time - 15 minutes **Cooking Time - 20 minutes** **12 Bhature**

Ingredients

Flour : 1 cup
Curds : little less than ½ cup
Pinch of salt
Sugar : ½ tsp.
Ghee (melted) : 1 tsp.
Hot Water : 5 to 6 tbsp.
Oil or Vanaspati to fry

Method

(i) Warm the flour.
(ii) Sieve together the flour, salt and soda.
(iii) Add sugar, curds and water and knead to make a dough
(iv) Knead well.
(v) Apply the melted ghee and knead well again.
(vi) Keep in a warm place in a utensil and cover with a wet cloth.
(vii) Make 12 to 14 equal portions of the dough. Roll out 4 inch puris and fry till golden brown.
(viii) Serve hot with chole.

Aloo Parathe

Preparation Time - 20 minutes **Cooking Time - 30 to 40 minutes** **8 to 10 Parathas**

Ingredients

Flour : 1 ½ cups
Salt to taste
Oil : 2 tbsp.

Filling

Potatoes : 500 gms
Green Chillies : 2
Red Chilli Powder : 1 tsp.
Whole Coriander Powder : 1 ½ tbsp.
Dry Mango Powder : 1 ½ tbsp. or Lemon Juice
Chopped Coriander : ¼ cup
Salt to taste
Oil : 2 tbsp.
Cumin Seeds : ½ tsp.

Method

(i) To make dough add salt and oil to wheat flour and knead well.
(ii) Boil and peel potatoes. Chop them fine (or grate)
(iii) Cut the chillies fine.
(iv) Heat oil in a pan. Add cumin seeds and chillies. Stir Then add whole coriander powder, salt, red chilli powder and dry mango powder and sauté well.
(v) Later add the chopped potatoes and mix well.
(vi) Mash the mixture well with your hands.
(vii) Add coriander and mix well.
(viii) Divide the mixture into 8 to 10 equal portions. Divide the dough into equal no. of balls.
(ix) Roll out each ball into a four inch roti. Place 1 portion of the potato mixture in the centre of the roti. Close the mouth of the ball and roll out the paratha. Roll out the others in the same way.
(x) Smear a little oil on gridle while roasting parathas to a golden brown colour.
(xi) Serve the parathas hot with curds.

Cauliflower Paratha

Preparation Time - 15 minutes **Cooking Time - 30 minutes** **12 Parathas**

Ingredients

Cauliflower : 250 gms (without stalks)
Salt, Sugar, Lemon Juice and Green Chilli Paste according to taste
A little finely Chopped Coriander
Grated Coconut : ¼ cup
Wheat Flour : 2 cups
Oil : 2 tbsp.
Salt to taste
Ghee or Oil to roast parathas

Method

(i) Add oil (mohan) and salt to the flour & knead to form a medium soft dough.
(ii) Peel the stalks, grate the florets and the stalks.
(iii) Add coconut, coriander, salt, chilli paste, sugar and lemon juice to the grated cauliflower and mix well.
(iv) Make 24 equal portions of the dough.
(v) Roll out puris which are thickish and big in size.
(vi) On one puri spread the stuffing thinly. Now place the second puri on top of this one. Press the edges so that there is no opening on any side. If you feel that the edges need trimming then do so with a knife.
(vii) Put ghee or oil on a hot tava (skillet) and roast till golden brown. Serve hot.

Rotis in Mango Pulp

Preparation Time - 10 minutes **Cooking Time - 30 minutes** **6 to 8 Rotis**

Ingredients

Condensed Mango Pulp : 1 cup
Mava : 100 gms
Castor Sugar : according to taste
Whole Wheat Flour : 1 cup
Besan : 1 tsp.
Oil : 2 tsp.

Method

(i) Mix the sugar, mava and pulp together to make a soft mixture.
(ii) Add oil and besan to the whole wheat flour and prepare a mixture identical in softness to the mango pulp.
(iii) Divide the mango pulp mixture into small balls (the size of a small lemon).
(iv) Make balls out of the whole wheat flour mixture. They should be double in quantity compared to the mango pulp balls.
(v) Place a flattened mango mixture ball between two flattened wheat flour balls. Roll out into rotis. Roast on a skillet.
(vi) These rotis last well for 8 days.

Dal Puri

Preparation Time - 15 minutes **Cooking Time - 30 minutes** **16 to 18 Puris**

Ingredients

Whole Wheat Floor : 2 cups
Oil : 2 to 3 tbsp.
Salt to taste
Pinch of Turmeric
Water to prepare a dough

Filling

Split Black Beans : 1 cup
Cinnamon Powder : 1 tsp. (level)
Cloves Powder : 1 tsp. (level)
Cumin Powder : 1 tsp.
Red Chilli Powder : 1 tsp. (level)
Garam Masala : ½ tsp.
Oil : 3 tbsp.
Cumin Seeds : ½ tsp.
Salt to taste

Method

(i) Add salt and oil (mohan) to whole wheat flour and prepare a dough.
(ii) Soak the split black beans in water for 5 to 6 hours.
(iii) Wash and clean the dal well. Cook it in a pressure cooker with water, salt and turmeric powder. (The dal should remain whole)
(iv) After one whistle lower the flame and shut off the gas after 3 minutes.
(v) Drain the dal in a collander to remove the water completely. It should be dry.
(vi) Heat oil in a pan. Add cumin seeds and dal.
(vii) Add salt, remaining powders and red chilli powder. Mix together and cover the pan and let it cook for some time.
(viii) Make 16 to 17 equal portions of the whole wheat flour dough.
(ix) Make similar numbers of equal portions of the filling.
(x) Roll out the ball a little. Place the filling in the centre. Seal the mouth of the ball.
(xi) Roll out thick puris and fry till golden brown. These puris are good as a breakfast dish and are also very nutritious.

Carrot Tomato Puris

Preparation Time - 15 minutes **Cooking Time - 20 minutes** **75 Puris**

Ingredients

Tomatoes : 100 gms (red)
Carrots : 100 gms (Delhi variety)
Oil : 3 tbsp.
Red Chilli Powder and
Salt to taste
Whole Wheat Flour : 2 to
2 ½ cups

Method

(i) Make tomato puree (refer method no. : 3).
(ii) Extract carrot juice.
(iii) Add salt and red chilli powder.
(iv) If the tomatoes are not very red, then you can add 4 drops of tomato red colour to improve it.
(v) Add oil (mohan) to the whole wheat flour and prepare a stiff dough.
(vi) Roll out puris and fry in oil.

Ukadi Rotis

Preparation Time - 15 minutes **Cooking Time - 30 minutes** **5 to 6 Rotis**

Ingredients

Maida : ¼ cup (heaped)
Whole Wheat Flour : ¼ cup (level)
Salt to taste
Oil : 3 tbsp.

Ukad

Rice Flour : 1 cup (full)
Oil : 1 tbsp.
Salt to taste
Water : 1 cup

Method

(i) Mix the flour and whole wheat flour together.
(ii) Add salt and 1 tbsp. oil to the flour and make a soft dough with water.

Ukad

(i) Bring to boil water, oil and salt. After it boils remove from gas. To this, add rice, flour and mix and blend this mixture well.
(ii) Place the pan on the gas with a cover. Reduce the heat.
(iii) Let it cook well and then turn off the gas.
(iv) Place the ukad in a plate. To this apply water or oil and knead it well so that it becomes soft and pliable.
(v) To the dough add 2 tbsp. oil and water (as required) and knead well. The consistency of this dough should be like the Puran-Poli dough.
(vi) Proceed as you would for puran-poli preparation. Only instead of puran fill ukad in the centre, lift edges, seal the centre and roll out the roti.
(vii) These rotis are excellent with aamras (mango pulp) as an accompaniment. Serve these rotis lukewarm.

Important Note : *It is preferable to use Basmati rice or any other variety with a good aroma. Wash and drain the rice. Dry in shade and grind to flour.*

Methi Paratha

Preparation Time - 15 minutes **Cooking Time - 20 times** **6 Parathas**

Ingredients

Finely Chopped Methi (fenugreek) : 1 cup
Gram Flour : 1 cup
Whole Wheat Flour : ½ cup
Onion : 1 (medium)
Chillies : 2 (green)
Red Chilli Powder : ½ to 1 tsp.
Ajwain : ½ tsp. (pounded)
Oil : 2 to 3 tbsp. (mohan)
Salt according to taste
Oil to fry Parathas

Method

(i) Chop the onion fine or grate it.
(ii) Cut the chillies fine.
(iii) Mix together methi, onion, chillies, salt, both the flours, other masalas and oil (mohan). With the help of water prepare a dough that is stiff in consistency.
(iv) Make 6 equal portions of the above mixture.
(v) Roll out each portion into a small round roti, apply oil and proceed to fold them like parathas. Now roll out thick parathas. Put oil on the skillet. Cook till golden brown.
(vi) Serve hot with curds.

Khasta Paratha

Preparation Time - 15 minutes **Cooking Time - 30 times** **6 to 7 Parathas**

Ingredients

Gram Flour : ¾ cup
Wheat Flour : ½ cup
Green Chillies : 1 to 2
Finely Chopped Onion : ¼ cup full
Ajwain or Carrom Seeds : ¼ tsp.
Pomegranate Seeds : 20 (optional)
Red Chilli Powder : ¼ tsp.
Turmeric Powder : ¼ tsp.
Salt as per taste
Oil : 2 tbsp.
Chopped Coriander : ¼ cup

Method

(i) Mix gram and wheat flour together.
(ii) Chop the chillies fine.
(iii) Add oil to the gram-wheat flour mixture and apply it well to the flour.
(iv) Add all remaining ingredients to the flour. With the help of water knead a soft dough. Cover and keep aside for ½ an hour.
(v) Divide dough to 6 to 7 equal parts.
(vi) Take one part and roll out a puri. Apply oil to it and sprinkle rice flour over it. Fold it. Apply oil on the fold and sprinkle rice flour. Fold again. Roll out a thickish paratha with the help of rice flour (1/8" thick). Grease pan with oil. Roast paratha on the medium flame till golden brown on both sides. Serve it hot.

Important Note : *You can serve curds, chunda or butter with this. This paratha can be served along with meals or even as a quick snack.*

Bajari Paratha

Preparation Time - 10 minutes **Cooking Time - 20 minutes** **6 to 8 Parathas**

Ingredients

Bajri Flour : 1 cup full
Finely Chopped Onion : 2 tbsp.
Green Chilli : 1
Red Chilli Powder : ¼ tsp.
Pomegranate Seeds : 15 seeds (optional)
Salt as per taste
Homemade Ghee

Method

(i) Mix all ingredients together except ghee. With the help of water, knead a dough for parathas.

(ii) Roll out a paratha of $1/8$" thickness. Roast paratha on pan with ghee on both sides. Serve it hot.

Important Note : *Make sure the bajri flour is fresh. If the flour is not fresh then it tastes bitter.*

Pulav

This dish that was very commonly prepared in U. P. and Punjab has today become a hot favourite all over the country. In Maharashtra the 'Masala Bhaat' is very commonly prepared during auspicious occasions. This is a customary practice. This preparation is quite spicy and does not need to be served with other curries. Since the rice itself contains many masalas, you cannot serve this with other spicy dishes.

With a pulav you can serve a variety of curries and enjoy the taste. Basically, if the pulav is mild other spicy dishes can provide a good combination and go well together. Use of Basmati rice, not only with its aroma, long and fine grains makes the preparation look good but, it also tastes good.

Some Important Tips :

(i) Wash the rice and drain atleast ½ an hour before preparing the pulav.
(ii) Saute the rice, lightly so that the grains don't break.
(iii) The rice for the pulav should be cooked in such a way that each grain is separate.
(iv) While preparing pulav or plain rice the amount of water required depends on whether the rice is new or old. New rice requires less water whereas old rice requires more water.
(v) When the rice is almost ready don't stir.
(vi) For decoration on the pulav, use finely chopped coriander or fried onion slices.
(vii) For the pulav, the rice can be sauted on ghee or oil (as mentioned in the recipe).
You can prepare the rice directly in a vessel or in a pressure cooker as per your convenience. While preparing rice in the cooker, for the grains to remain separate, you have to decide the amount of time it has to be kept after the whistle goes. Normally in the cooker you will require little more than double the water.

Spring Onion Pulav

Preparation Time - 15 minutes **Cooking Time - 15 minutes** **Serves : 6**

Ingredients

Basmati Rice : 1 cup
Garam Masala : ½ tsp.
(Refer masalas section)
Onion : 1 (medium size)
Spring Onions : 3
Tomato : 1 (medium) optional
Oil : 3 tbsp.
Potato : 1 (big size)
Bread : 1 slice
Coriander : ¼ cup (finely chopped)
Green Chilli : 1
Lemon Juice : 1 tsp.
Oil to fry Onion : 1 (medium size)
Salt to taste

Method

(i) Wash and drain the rice.
(ii) Slice onions finely.
(iii) Slice the spring onions and chop the shoots (green leaves) fine.
(iv) If you decide to use tomato, chop it finely.
(v) Heat oil in a skillet. First add the slices of onion. Saute till they change colour and become yellowish. Later add the spring onions along with its chopped leaves and saute.
(vi) Add the rice and saute well.
(vii) After adding salt and garam masala add water and cook the rice. Each grain of the cooked rice should be separate.
(viii) Boil potatoes till soft and mash.
(ix) Soak the slice of bread in water.
(x) Chop the onion and chilli fine.
(xi) Squeeze out water from the bread and add it to the mashed potato. Add lemon juice, salt, onion, chilli and mix together.
(xii) Make small pea-size balls. Fry till they are brownish .
(xiii) Loosen the cooked rice lightly with moist hands. After warming it, add the fried balls and mix well. Before serving sprinkle chopped coriander on top.

Methi (Fenugreek) Pulav

Preparation Time - 10 minutes **Cooking Time - 40 minutes** **Serves : 6**

Ingredients

Basmati Rice : 1 cup
Fenugreek Seeds : 1 ½ tbsp.
Garlic Cloves : 8 (large)
Green Chillies : 3
Salt to taste
Oil : 2 to 3 tbsp.
Mustard, Asafoetida and Turmeric
Dry Coconut : 2 inches (piece)
Cumin Seeds : 1 tsp.
Ghee : pure ghee

Method

(i) Soak the methi seeds in water for 8 to 9 hours.
(ii) After it is soaked well drain in a collander. When it becomes a little dry tie it in a cloth for it to sprout.
(iii) When the methi sprouts it is ready to be used in the pulav.
(iv) Wash the rice and keep aside.
(v) Crush the garlic a little.
(vi) Slice the chillies into long thin pieces.
(vii) Roast the dry coconut on open fire till it turns black.
(viii) Pound the dry coconut and the cumin seeds fine.
(ix) Heat oil in a skillet. To this add mustard, asafoetida and turmeric and stir. Now add the garlic, chillies and saute.
(x) Add the (½ cup) methi (sprouted) and the rice and stir. Add salt, the ground masalas & cook the rice. When the rice is still hot, pour some ghee.

Cheese Pulav

Preparation Time - 30 minutes **Cooking Time - 25 minutes** **Serves : 6**

Ingredients

Rice : 1 cup (Basmati)
French Beans : 50 gms
Carrots : 50 gms
Florettes : 50 gms (cauliflower)
Peas : 50 gms
Potato : 1 (medium)
Tomato : 1 (medium)
Chillies : 2 (green)
Ginger : ½ inch
Coriander Powder : 2 tsp.
Salt to taste
Oil : 2 tbsp.
Onion : 1 (medium)

White Sauce

Milk : 1 cup (hot)
Butter : 2 tsp. (level)
Flour : 2 tsp.
Salt and Pepper to taste
Grated Cheese : 4 tbsp.

Method

(i) Wash the rice well and keep aside
(ii) Saute rice in ghee and prepare the rice. Each grain should be separate.
(iii) Cut the vegetables into medium pieces. Boil the peas vegetables in water with a pinch of soda.
(iv) Boil and peel the potatoes and cut into small pieces.
(v) Chop onion, ginger and green chillies fine.
(vi) Chop the tomato.
(vii) Heat oil in a skillet. Saute onion, ginger and chillies till light brown.
(viii) Add coriander powder and tomato and stir. Add salt.
(ix) Add the vegetables and lemon juice.
(x) Prepare white sauce (see method no.: 5).
(xi) After the sauce is ready, remove from the gas. Add ½ portion grated cheese, salt and pepper and mix together.
(xii) Mix the rice lightly in the white sauce.
(xiii) In an oven proof dish (1-2" deep, oval or any other shape) grease the inside of the bowl with butter. Spread the vegetable mixture and press lightly. Then spread the rice layer and the remaining grated cheese.
(xiv) Bake in an oven at 150°C for 20 minutes.

Palak (Spinach) Carrot Pulav

Preparation Time - 20 minutes **Cooking Time - 15 minutes** **Serves : 6**

Ingredients

Basmati Rice : 1 cup
Spinach : 1 bunch
Carrot : 1 (English)
Salt to taste
Masala used is same as in Double Beans Pulav (Page no. 16)

Method

(i) Wash and drain the rice.
(ii) Grind palak leaves coarsely (in mixer).
(iii) Cut the carrot into small pieces.
(iv) Proceed ahead as per the Double Beans Pulav (page no. 16).

Kashmiri Pulav

Preparation Time - 20 minutes **Cooking Time - 20 minutes** **Serves : 6 to 8**

Ingredients

Basmati Rice : 250 gms
Peas : 100 gms (fresh)
Carrots : 100 gms (English)
Cherries : 25 gms (preserved)
Tutti Frooti : 25 gms
Pineapple slices : 2 (tinned)
Apple : 1 (small)
Lemon : ½
Salt to taste
Bay Leaves : 2 black
Cardamoms : 2
Pure Ghee : 2 tbsp.
(thick consistency)
Tomatoes : 2 (medium) puree
Artificial Red or
Orange colour : ½ tsp.

Masala to Grind

Onion : 2 (medium size)
Mint Leaves : handful
Garlic Cloves : 4
Ginger : ½ inch
Black Cumin : ½ tsp.
Fennel Seeds : ½ tsp.
Whole Coriander : 1 tsp.
Cloves : 4
Cinnamon : 4 pieces (1")
Kashmiri Red Chillies : 6
Oil : 4 tbsp.
Salt to taste

For Decoration

Onion : 1 (medium)
Cashewnuts : 50 gms
Finely chopped Coriander

Method

(i) Wash and drain the rice an hour in advance and keep aside.
(ii) Ten minutes before cooking the rice, apply lemon juice and salt to it.
(iii) Grate the carrots.
(iv) Cut each cherry into four pieces.
(v) Wash the tutti-frooti and dry them.
(vi) Cut the apple and pineapple into pieces.
(vii) In a skillet heat the oil. Add bay leaves, black cardamom and let it sizzle. Now add the peas, carrot and rice and saute. After adding salt and water prepare the rice in a pressure cooker (10 minutes).
(viii) Saute the ground masala in oil along with the tomato puree (method no. : 3) Add salt.
(ix) Saute the fruits in little ghee.
(x) Slice the onion and fry in oil till brown. Brown the Cashewnuts in ghee.
(xi) The grains of the cooked rice should be separate. Apply the artificial colours to the rice lightly. Mix the sauted fruits and masala to the rice.
(xii) Grease the vessel. Spread pulav in it. Keep in an oven or steam in cooker. This is just for heating.
(xiii) Decorate the rice with fried onion and cashewnuts. Sprinkle chopped coriander.

Crispy Pulav

Preparation Time - 30 minutes **Cooking time - 20 minutes** **Serves : 6**

Ingredients

Amul Butter (softened) : 1 tbsp.
Amul Cheese Cube : 1
Cornflakes : 1 ½ cups
Milk : 1 cup (8 to 10 ounces)
Bay Leaves : 1
Mace : 1
Oil : 1 tbsp.
Onion : 1 (medium size)
Basmati Rice : 1 cup (level)
Cauliflower : 400 gms
Amul Butter : 2 tbsp.
Flour : 2 tbsp. (level)
Salt and Pepper to taste

Method

(i) Take an oven-proof dish of good depth with a capacity of 5 to 6 cups of water.
(ii) Melt the butter and grease the dish with it.
(iii) Grate the cheese. Crush the cornflakes a little and mix together.
(iv) Spread 1 cup of the above mixture on the bottom of the greased oven proof dish. Press lightly.
(v) To the milk add the mace and the bay leaves. Let it boil on low flame and keep it aside.
(vi) Chop the onion fine.
(vii) In a skillet add oil and saute the onions (do not allow the colour to change).
(viii) Add the washed rice and stir. Add salt to taste and prepare rice each grain should be separate.
(ix) Boil the florettes in water (do not make them too soft).
(x) Prepare white sauce (thin consistency) with milk (strained), butter, flour and ½ cup water (refer method no. : 5). Add salt and pepper.
(xi) Spread rice in the greased dish. Pour half the sauce on it and then the florettes. Pour the remaining sauce. Then spread the cornflakes mixture. Bake for 10 minutes at 150°C.

***Important Note :** Serve tomato saar with this pulav*

Peas Pulav

Preparation Time - 10 minutes **Cooking Time - 15-20 minutes** **Serves : 6**

Ingredients

Basmati Rice : 1 cup
Peas : 1 cup
Pinch of Soda
Salt to taste
Cumin Seeds : ¼ tsp.
Bay Leaves : 1
Cloves : 4
Cinnamon Sticks : 1 (piece)
Ghee : 1 tbsp.

Method

(i) Pick and wash the rice and drain at least ½ an hour in advance.
(ii) Boil the peas adding pinch of soda to it.
(iii) Heat ghee in a skillet. Add cumin seeds, and the remaining masalas. Saute well. Add the rice and continue stirring lightly. Add salt and water. The cooked rice grains should be separate.
(iv) Gently mix the rice and peas together.
(v) On a low flame steam this for some time.

Vegetable Biryani

Preparation time - 30 minutes **Cooking time - 30 minutes** **Serves : 6**

Ingredients
Basmati Rice : 1 cup
Bay Leaves : 2
Cinnamon : 3 pieces
Green Cardamom : 4
Salt to taste
Ghee : 1 tbsp.

Vegetable Korma
French Beans : 50 gms
Carrots (English) : 50 gms
Peas : 50 gms (shelled)
Potatoes : 2 (medium)
Curds : 1 cup
Saffron : 10 threads
Milk : 1 tbsp.
Lemon Juice : 2 tbsp.
Salt to taste
Ghee : 2 tbsp.
Onions : 2 (medium size)

Masala to grind
Onions : 2 (medium size)
Ginger : 1 inch piece
Garlic : 6 cloves
Mint : 4 springs
Coriander : a handful
Cumin Seeds : ½ tsp.
Black Cumin : ½ tsp.
Turmeric : ¼ tsp.
Whole Coriander : 2 tsp.
Red Chillies : 3

For Decoration
Cashewnuts : 50 gms

Method
(i) Wash the rice ½ an hour in advance and keep aside.
(ii) Saute all the masalas well in ghee. Add rice and saute for some time. Prepare rice by adding salt and water. Each grain should be separate.

Korma
(i) Cut the french beans in fine diagonal pieces.
(ii) Cut the carrots in small pieces.
(iii) Beat the curds. Soak the chopped vegetables and peas in the curds for ½ and hour.
(iv) Fry potato chips.
(v) Slice the onion fine and fry in oil till brown.
(vi) Add saffron to lukewarm milk.
(vii) Heat ghee in a skillet. Saute ground masala in it. Now add the vegetables soaked in curds and cook. If needed add some water. Let the vegetables retain some liquid.
(viii) Add salt.
(ix) Fry cashewnuts.
(x) Apply ghee to a vessel. Spread half the rice in it. Spread the vegetables on it. On this spread fried potatoes and half the fried onions.
(xi) Spread the remaining rice and press lightly.
(xii) Sprinkle saffron soaked milk and lemon juice and cover the vessel. Set your oven at 150°C and bake for 15 minutes.
(xiii) Before serving decorate with remaining fried onions and fried cashewnuts.

Orange Delight, Caramel Custard, Pineapple Pudding

Fruit Chaat and Orange Onion Salad

Parsi Pulav

Preparation Time - 10 minutes **Cooking Time - 20 minutes** **Serves : 6**

Ingredients

Basmati Rice : 1 cup
Onion : 1 (medium)
Cloves : 4
Green Cardamoms : 4
Cinnamon : 2 pieces (1 inch)
Ghee : 1 tbsp.
Salt to taste
Sugar : 1 tbsp.
Water : 1 tbsp.

Method

(i) Wash the rice and keep it aside.
(ii) Chop the onion finely.
(iii) Heat the ghee in a skillet. When it is hot add the onion and saute till dark brown.
(iv) Add cloves, cinnamon and green cardamom and stir for sometime.
(v) Add the rice and stir. After adding salt and enough water bring to boil and reduce the heat.
(vi) In a thick bottom vessel add water and sugar and prepare the caramel (see method no.: 4). Add it to the rice that is being cooked, mix together and prepare the rice.

***Important Note :** This pulav can be served with Dhansak (Refer to the curry section)*

Tomato Pulav

Preparation Time - 25 minutes **Cooking Time - 10 minutes** **Serves : 6**

Ingredients

Basmati Rice : 1 cup
Coconut : ½ (small size)
Tomatoes : 2 (medium size)
Kishmish : 1 tbsp.
Garam Masala : (whole pieces - cloves, green cardamom, bay leaves, cinnamon)
Sugar : ½ tsp.
Salt to taste
Ghee : 1 tsp.

Masala to grind

Coriander : 1 handful
Green Chillies : 2
Turmeric : ¼ tsp.

For Decoration

Onion - 1 (medium size)
Cashewnuts - 1 handful

Method

(i) Pick and wash the rice. Keep aside.
(ii) Place the tomatoes in hot water. Remove the skin and make puree (see method no. : 1).
(iii) Extract coconut milk.
(iv) Apply the masala paste to the washed rice.
(v) Cut the onion in long thin slices.
(vi) Fry sliced onion, cashewnuts and kishmish separately in oil or ghee till brown. Keep aside.
(vii) Heat ghee in a vessel. Add the garam masala. When it begins to splutter add the rice and stir.
(viii) Add the tomato puree, coconut milk, water and salt to taste and sugar. Prepare the rice.
(ix) Before serving decorate with the fried onion, cashewnuts and kishmish.

Masoor Pulav

Preparation Time - 15 minutes **Cooking Time - 15 minutes** **Serves : 6**

Ingredients

Basmati Rice : 1 cup
Masoor (whole) : ½ cup
Ghee : 1 tbsp. (thick)
Cumin Seeds : ¼ tsp.
Salt to taste
Bay Leaves : 2
Cloves : 4
Cinnamon : 2 pieces
Green Cardamoms : 3

Method

(i) Soak the masoor for 4 to 5 hours in water and drain. Then transfer it into a collander to drain.
(ii) Pick and wash the rice and drain.
(iii) Heat the ghee in a skillet and add all the masalas. When it begins to splutter add the masoor and stir. Now add the rice and continue stirring. Add hot water, salt and cook.

Double Beans Pulav

Preparation Time - 15 minutes **Cooking Time - 20 minutes** **Serves : 6**

Ingredients

Basmati Rice : 1 cup
Fresh Double Beans : 100 gms
Salt to taste
Oil : 2 to 3 tbsp.
Ghee : 2 tbsp. (melted)

Masala to Grind

Onion : 1 (large)
Ginger : 1 inch
Garlic : 10
Green Chillies : 1 to 2
Cloves : 3
Black Pepper : 3
Cinnamon : 1 ½ inch piece
Whole Coriander : 1 tsp.
Cumin Seeds : 1 tsp.
Bay Leaves : 1

Method

(i) Wash the rice and keep it aside.
(ii) Parboil the double beans.
(iii) Heat the oil in the skillet. Add the masala paste and saute well. Sprinkle some water.
(iv) Add the beans and saute.
(v) Add the rice and stir
(vi) Add salt and water. Cook the rice.
(vii) Before serving the rice, pour a little ghee on it.

Important Note : *When double beans are out of season, you can use the dried double beans. Soak the dried ones in water, overnight.*

Vadi Pulav

Preparation Time - 15 minutes **Cooking Time - 15 minutes** **Serves : 6**

Ingredients

Basmati Rice : 1 cup
Onion : 1 (medium)
Amritsari Whole Black Beans
Vadi : 1
Salt to taste
Oil : 1 tbsp.
Ghee : 1 tbsp.

Method

(i) Pick and wash the rice. Keep it aside.
(ii) Make small pieces of the vadi. Saute them in oil. Add some water and cook them. Do not throw away the water.
(iii) Chop the onion fine.
(iv) Heat the ghee. Saute the onions in it. Then saute the rice.
(v) Add salt to taste, the vadis along with the water plus some additional water and prepare rice.
(vi) This pulav tastes excellent with curds.

***Important Note :** The Amritsari whole black beans vadis are easily available in Sindhi Stores.*

Roman Rice

Preparation Time - 15 minutes **Cooking Time - 20 minutes** **Serves : 6**

Ingredients

Basmati Rice : 1 cup
Double Beans Seeds : 1 cup fresh or ½ cup dried
Carrots : 100 gms.
Tomato : 1 (medium)
Onion : 1 (medium)
Chopped Coriander : ¼ cup
Basil Leaves or Sprigs : 1 tsp.
Grated Cheese : 1 cup
Amul Butter : 2 tbsp.
Garlic Cloves : 4 (large crushed)
Pepper : ¼ to ½ tsp.
Salt to taste
Oil : 2 tbsp.

Method

(i) If you are using dried double beans, then soak them overnight.
(ii) Cook the double beans till they are soft.
(iii) Pick and wash the rice. Add salt and cook the rice.
(iv) When the rice is still hot, loosen it and add the grated cheese and butter. Mix lightly.
(v) Chop the onion fine.
(vi) Chop the tomato into small pieces.
(vii) Cut carrots into small pieces.
(viii) Crush the basil.
(ix) Heat the oil in a skillet. To it add the onion, coriander, basil, carrots, garlic and saute till the onion turns light brown in colour. See that the carrot is cooked too.
(x) Now add the tomato, double beans, salt and pepper.
(xi) Now mix the above mixture and rice lightly. Cover and reheat it.

Bishi Byali Anna

Preparation Time - 10 minutes **Cooking Time - 20 minutes** **Serves : 4 to 6**

Ingredients

Rice : 1 cup (not basmati)
Toor Dal : 1 cup
Salt to taste
White Sesame Seeds : 2 tbsp.
Dry Coconut : 2" / 2"
Sambar Masala : 1 ½ tsp.
(Refer masala section no. : 1)
Red Chilli Powder : ½ tsp.
Salt to taste
Tamarind : size of a big lemon
Jaggery : size of a small beetle- nut
Red Chillies : 4
Curry Leaves : 15 to 20
Melted-Ghee : 6 tbsp.
(homemade)

Method

(i) Mix the rice and dal together and wash it well.
(ii) Cook the rice till soft in a pressure cooker with salt. A little more than double water.
(iii) Soak the tamarind in water.
(iv) Roast the sesame seeds and pound to a powder.
(v) Make pieces of the red chillies.
(vi) Roast the coconut piece on open fire till it turns black. Then pound it.
(vii) Make a pulp out of the soaked tamarind.
(viii) Beat the cooked rice and dal together.
(ix) Place the skillet on the gas. Add the tamarind pulp along with ½ cup water. Add salt, chilli powder, sambar masala and the sesame and coconut powder. Add 5 to 6 curry leaves and let it boil well. Add 2 cups water and let it boil again. Now add the beaten dal and rice and mix well together. Cook further on a low flame. If required add water. Add the jaggery.
(x) Heat little ghee. Add chillies and curry leaves and add this to the above mixture.
(xi) Serve hot.

***Important Note** :This dish should have a pouring consistency.*

***Try this** :* *To decorate glasses for sherbets, juices or cold drinks : Beat the egg whites a little. On the upper edge of the glass apply some of this mixture. Then roll it in icing sugar or in coloured sugar. It looks good.*

Curries and Vegetables

You will find the freshest vegetables in the four cold months of winter. The fact that all the vegetables whether in season or off are readily available in cities everyday of the year is another story. Today we are exposed to different varieties of food of various communities. People go to restaurants serving exotic dishes or are invited by their friends for parties. Our taste-buds are exposed to a variety of dishes and we often find them delicious and appealing. But everyone cannot afford the expenses incurred while eating out. Hence more and more people now prefer to prepare many dishes served in restaurants at home.

While preparing any curry or vegetables certain things should be kept in mind.

(i) As far as possible ensure that the vegetables are fresh.

(ii) If the vegetables are stored in the fridge then before cooking they should be kept out for an hour at least.

(iii) Cut the vegetables in equal shapes as far as possible.

(iv) If the vegetables have to be boiled for a particular recipe then while doing so add a pinch of soda. This helps the vegetables to retain maximum of there natural colour plus to boil well.

(v) In a Punjabi dish chop the onion very fine. Or you can grate it. The onion should be sauted till it turns brown, the curry will taste better.

(vi) Before adding the red chilli powder remove the vessel from the heat. After stirring, place it back on the gas. Then the colour of the chillies remains intact.

(vii) Use refined oil. Continue sauting till the ingredient releases oil.

(viii) Grind the masalas to a paste.

(ix) It is very handy to keep ground green chillies, ginger and garlic in different jars in the fridge. Then they are readily available when you need them.

Bihari Dal

Preparation Times : 5 minutes **Cooking Time : 20 minutes** **Serves : 4 to 6**

Ingredients

Toor Dal : 1 cup
Turmeric : ¼ tsp.
Mango (raw) : 50 gms
Salt to taste
Garlic Cloves : 6 to 8
Red Chillies : 6 to 8
Asafoetida Powder : ½ tsp.
Melted Ghee : 4 tbsp. (homemade)
Chopped Coriander

Method

(i) Wash the toor dal and cook till soft in a pressure cooker. Add turmeric and asafoetida powder while cooking.
(ii) Peel and cut raw mangoes into pieces.
(iii) Crush the garlic. Cut the chillies into 1" pieces.
(iv) Beat the dal, but not to a paste. Add the raw mangoes along with some water in a skillet and boil it a little, till it becomes somewhat soft. Then add the dal. Let it boil for some time so that the sourness of the mango is transferred to the dal. Add salt.
(vi) Heat the ghee in a small vessel. Add garlic and chillies. When the garlic turns brownish add it to the cooked dal. Garnish with coriander.

Important Note : *Let the consistency of this dal be thick. Plain rice provides a nice combination with this dal. While having this dal with rice crush the chillies in it with your hand.*

Masoor Curry

Preparation Time : 10 minutes **Cooking Time : 15 minutes** **Serves : 4**

Ingredients

Masoor (whole) : ½ cup
Tamarind : size of a beetlenut
Salt to taste
Oil : 2 tbsp.
To temper : Mustard, Asafoetida and Turmeric

Masalas to grind

Grated Fresh Coconut
2 to 3 tbsp.
Chopped Coriander : ¼ cup
Green chillies : 2 to 3
Garlic Cloves : 8

Method

(i) Soak the masoor overnight.
(ii) Heat the oil in a skillet. Add mustard, turmeric and asafoetida. Add the masoor and stir.
(iii) Add water and parboil it. Now add the ground masala and salt and cook till done.
(iv) Soak tamarind in little water. When it softens, squeeze the tamarind and use the extract. Add it to the above dal mixture.

Important Note : *Even though the masoor is completely cooked, the grain should be whole. This curry is very tasty.*

Cabbage Kofta Curry

Preparation Time : 30 minutes **Cooking time : 30 minutes** **Serves : 6**

Ingredients

Cabbage : 500 gms
Besan : (gram flour) : 1 tbsp.
Soda : 2 pinches
Turmeric : ¼ tsp.
Coriander Powder : ½ tsp.
Red Chilli Powder : ½ tsp.
Garam Masala : ½ tsp.
Salt to taste
Oil for frying

Curry

Onions : 2 medium
Green Chillies : 2
Ginger : 1 inch
Curds : ½ litre (beaten)
Peas : ½ cup (optional)
Cumin Seeds : ¼ tsp.
Coriander Powder : 1 tsp.
Salt to taste
Garam Masala : ½ tsp.
(Refer to method no. : 1)
Oil : 4 tbsp.
Chopped Coriander

Method (Koftas)

(i) Grate the cabbage.
(ii) Add soda, salt, turmeric, chilli powder, coriander powder garam masala and besan to the grated cabbage. Mix and make koftas.
(iii) Deep fry in oil till golden brown.

Curry

(i) Cut chillies into long slices.
(ii) Cut ginger into juliens/fine shreds.
(iii) Grate the onions.
(iv) If you choose to use the peas, then boil them first.
(v) Heat oil in a skillet. Add cumin seeds, chillies, ginger and onion. Saute till brownish.
(vi) Remove from heat and add turmeric, coriander powder and red chilli powder and stir.
(vii) After it cools add the beaten curds and place on the gas. Stir continuously. When it begins to boil add salt.
(viii) Bring to boil by adding 1 ½ to 2 cups water. Then if you want, add the peas. Add the koftas. Bring to boil. Remove from heat and add garam masala. Garnish with chopped coriander.

***Important Note :** Before serving add the koftas and bring to boil. Don't boil repeatedly or the koftas will break.*

Sol Kadhi (Kokum)

Preparation Time : 15 minutes **Cooking Time : 10 minutes** **Serves : 6**

Ingredients

Kokum : 10 to 12
Water : 1 cup
Coconut : 1 (small)
Masala to Grind
Green Chillies : 2 to 3
Garlic Cloves : 3
Chopped Coriander : ¼ cup
Salt to taste
Sugar to taste
Curry Leaves : 8 (chopped)
Cochinal Red Colour : 2 to 3 drops

Method

(i) Soak the kokum in water for 1 hour.
(ii) Remove the pieces from the water without crushing them.
(iii) Grate the coconut and extract coconut milk both thick and thin.
(iv) Combine together the coconut milk, kokum extract and add the ground masalas (grind the chillies, garlic and coriander to a paste). Add salt, sugar and chopped curry leaves.
(v) Do not heat this kadhi. No need of 'fodni' or 'tadka' either (refer to glossary).
(vi) Remove the curry leaves.
(vii) Add artificial colour.

Fresh Peas (Aamti) Curry

Preparation Time : 15 minutes **Cooking Time : 10 minutes** **Serves : 4 to 6**

Ingredients

Peas : 1 cup
Potato : 1 (medium)
Tamarind : (beetlenut size)
Jaggery : (more than tamarind)
Salt to taste
Oil : 2 tbsp.
Mustard Seeds, Asafoetida powder
Turmeric powder : $^1/_8$ tsp.
each

Masala to Grind

Grated Coconut : ¼ cup
Chopped Coriander : ¼ cup
Green Chilli : 1
Cloves : 2 to 3
Cinnamon : 1 ½ inch
Cumin Seeds : 1 tsp.

For thickening

Water : 2 tbsp.
Gram Flour (besan) : 1 tsp.

Method

(i) Boil the peas till soft.
(ii) Boil the potatoes and cut to pieces.
(iii) Soak the tamarind in water and make a pulp.
(iv) Add oil to a skillet. Add mustard, asafoetida and turmeric powders.
(v) Add the slightly mashed peas and potatoes and saute.
(vi) Add the ground masalas, salt, water, jaggery and tamarind and bring to boil.
(vii) To 2 tbsp. water add 1 tsp. besan. Mix it well. Add it to the mixture. Bring to boil.
(ix) This curry has to be thickish.

Koftas in Dudhi (Bottlegourd) Gravy

Preparation Time : 15 to 20 minutes Cooking Time : 30 minutes Serves : 4

Ingredients

Koftas

Bread : 6 slices
Flour : 3 tbsp.
Curds : ½ cup (beaten)
Soda : 2 pinches
Green Chillies : 2 to 3
Chopped Coriander
Salt to taste
Oil to fry.

Gravy

Onions : 200 gms
Peas : 1 cup (optional)
Tomatoes : 150 gms (2 medium)
Curds : 1 cup (not sour)
Red Chilli Powder : 1 tsp.
Coriander Powder : 1 tbsp.
Turmeric : ¼ tsp.
Garam Masala : ½ tsp.
(Refer method no. : 1)
Bottlegourds : 250 gms
Oil : 4 to 6 tbsp.

Garnish

Chopped Coriander

Method (Koftas)

(i) Cut out the sides of the bread and soak in the curds for 20 minutes.
(ii) Chop the green chillies.
(iii) To the bread add the flour, chillies, soda, salt and chopped coriander and make a mixture. Add little water if needed.
(iv) Make the koftas and deep fry.

Gravy

(i) Grate the onions.
(ii) If you choose to use peas, then boil them.
(iii) Peel the gourd (dudhi), chop and boil to make a puree.
(iv) Make a tomato puree (refer method no. : 3).
(v) Heat oil in a skillet. Saute onions till brownish. Add the turmeric and coriander powder and saute.
(vi) Remove from gas and add red chilli powder. Saute and place on the gas again and stir.
(vii) Add tomato puree and stir.
(viii) Beat the curds. Add it along with the bottlegourd puree. Add salt and boil for sometime.
(ix) Add koftas and bring to boil. Add garam masala.
(x) Sprinkle chopped coriander.

Important Note : *It is alright to prepare gravy in advance. But fry the koftas 1 hour before serving, or before adding to the curry. Add the koftas to the curry just before serving and give two boils.*

Konkani Kadhi

Preparation Time : 10 minutes **Cooking Time : 10 minutes** **Serves : 4 to 6**

Ingredients

Buttermilk : 2 cups (thick)
Coconut Milk : 2 cups
Green Chillies : 3
Turmeric : 1/8 tsp.
Salt to taste
Gram Flour (besan) :1 tbsp.
Sugar : 1 tsp.
Curry Leaves : 1 sprig
Chopped Coriander
Cumin Seeds, Asafoetida
Powder 1/8 tsp. each
Melted Ghee : 1 tbsp.

Method

(i) Mix the buttermilk and coconut milk. To this add the gram-flour for thickening.
(ii) Add the chilli pieces, curry leaves, salt, sugar and turmeric powder and mix.
(iii) Place it on the gas and bring to boil.
(iv) Heat ghee, add cumin seeds and asafoetida powder, when it splutters pour over the above mixture.

Important Note : *For this recipe avoid using sour buttermilk or buttermilk from the fridge. It you wish to use butter milk from the fridge then let it remain outside for 1 hour before cooking.*

Potato Sponge Curry

Preparation Time : 15 minutes **Cooking Time : 15 minutes** **Serves : 4**

Ingredients

Potatoes : 250 gms (walnut size)
Cumin Powder : ½ tsp.
Turmeric Powder : ¼ tsp.
Coriander Powder :½ tsp.
Red Chilli Powder : ½ tsp.
Curds : ½ cup
Saffron : 10 to 12 sticks
Salt to taste
Oil to fry : oil 3 tbsp.

Masala to Grind

Onions : 2 (medium)
Garlic : 6 cloves
Ginger : ½ inch
Red Chillies : 4

Garnish

Chopped Coriander

Method

(i) Peel the potatoes and wash them well.
(ii) With the help of a fork prick the potatoes evenly on all sides till spongy. Soak in salt water. Before deep frying the potatoes spread them on a towel till the water drains out.
(iii) Deep fry till potatoes are light brown.
(iv) Beat the curds well and add crushed saffron.
(v) Heat oil in a skillet. Add ground masalas and stir. Add the potatoes and stir.
(vi) Add all the other dry masalas, beaten curds and salt. Let it cook. Add water but let the gravy remain thickish.
(vii) Garnish with chopped coriander.

Important Note : *If you want to speed up the cooking process, pressure cook the potatoes with the masalas, curds etc., for a minute after one whistle, instead of step (vi) as mentioned.*

Koyade

Preparation Time : 10 minutes **Cooking Time : 20 minutes** **Serves : 4**

Ingredients

Sweet and Sour Mangoes : 8 (raiwal)
Metkut : 1 tbsp.
(available in market)
Mustard Powder : 1 tsp.
(beaten in little water)
Jaggery, Red Chilli Powder and Salt to taste
Oil : 3 tbsp.
Mustard, Asafoetida and Turmeric and pinch of Red Chilly Powder for the Fodni (tadka)

Method

(i) Wash the mangoes well and boil them in water till they change colour.
(ii) When they cool, peel and squeeze the centre seeds a little. But let the seeds remain in the mango pulp itself.
(iii) Remove some of the pulp from the above mixture. Add red chilli powder, salt, jaggery and the beaten mustard powder. Crush the jaggery till it dissolves in the mixture completely. Add this to the mango mixture. Add metkut and mix.
(iv) Make a fodni by adding mustard, turmeric, asafoetida, pinch of red chilli powder and pour it over the above mixture.

Important Note : *This dish can be prepared only in the Mango Season. It is very delicious and at the same time not tedious and time consuming.*

Palak (Spinach) Kofta Curry

Preparation Time : 20 minutes **Cooking Time : 20 minutes** **Serves : 4 to 6**

Ingredients

Spinach : 1 bunch
Gram Flour (besan) : ½ cup
Mawa : 2 tbsp.
Turmeric : ¼ tsp.
Red Chilli Powder : ½ tsp.
Garam Masala : ½ tsp.
Coriander Powder : 1 tsp.
Curds : 2 tsp.
Salt to taste
Pinch of Soda

Curry

Onion : 1 (large)
Tomato : 1 (medium)
Garlic : 8 cloves
Ginger : 1 ½ inch
Coriander Powder : 2 tsp. full
Red Chilli Powder : 1 tsp.
Salt to taste
Garam Masala : 1 tsp.
(Refer method no. : 1)
Turmeric : ¼ tsp.
Full Cream Curds : 1 tbsp.
Oil : 6 tbsp.
Garnish
Chopped Coriander

Method (Koftas)

(i) Remove the stalks from the palak. Chop finely and without adding water, steam and cook it either outside or in a pressure cooker. When it cools, squeeze out excess water.

(ii) Add gram flour, mawa, salt and other masalas along with the curds and a pinch of soda. Mix well together and make koftas and deep fry in oil.

Curry

(i) Grate the onions. Make a tomato puree (refer method no. : 3).

(ii) Grind the ginger and garlic.

(iii) Beat the curds well and keep aside.

(iv) Heat oil in a skillet and saute onions till golden brown. Add the ginger and garlic and stir. Add turmeric and coriander powder and continue stirring. After adding red chilli powder and the tomato puree, stir a little and add some water and let it cook.

(v) Add salt & fullcream curds. Mix. Add water. See to it that the curry is not too thick or thin in consistency.

(vi) Add the garam masala, then the koftas. Boil it for some time.

(vii) Sprinkle coriander on top of this curry.

Punjabi Dal

Preparation Time : 10 minutes **Cooking Time : 20 minutes** **Serves : 4**

Ingredients

Toor Dal : 1 cup
Tomato : 1 (medium)
Onion : 1 (medium)
Finely Chopped Onion : 1 tbsp.
Ginger : 1 inch
Green Chillies : 3
Few Curry Leaves
Chopped Coriander : ¼ cup
Lemon Juice : 3 tbsp.
Turmeric : ¼ tsp.
Ghee (thick) : 1 tsp. (homemade)
Salt to taste

Method

(i) Pick and wash the dal.
(ii) Slice onions.
(iii) Chop the tomato fine.
(iv) Chop the chillies and ginger finely.
(v) Add the onion and tomato to the toor dal and boil and cook it. The dal should have a thick consistency.
(vi) Heat little ghee in a skillet. Add the onions, chillies, ginger and curry leaves to it. Then add the beaten dal.
(vii) Add turmeric and salt and give two boils.
(viii) Add the lemon juice.
(ix) Just before serving, melt the remaining ghee and pour on it.

Important Note : *The dal tastes excellent when served hot. It also compliments other spicy dishes as it self its not too spicy.*

Gujrathi Kadhi

Preparation Time : 10 minutes **Cooking Time : 15 minutes** **Serves : 4 to 6**

Ingredients

Buttermilk : 4 cups (thick)
Gram Flour (besan) : 1 tbsp.
Salt to taste
Sugar : 3 tsp.
Pinch of Turmeric Powder
Few Curry Leaves
Red Chillies : 6 (round variety)
Whole Coriander : 1 tsp.
Cinnamon : 2 pieces
Cloves : 6
Oil : 3 tbsp.

Method

(i) Mix the besan and buttermilk
(ii) Mix well after adding salt, sugar and turmeric
(iii) Heat oil in a skillet add the curry leaves and the other masalas and stir. Add the butter milk. Once the kadhi boils it is ready.

Important Note : *This kadhi tastes very different and delicious from the traditional kadhi preparation.*

Tomato Saar

Preparation Time : 20 minutes **Cooking Time : 10 minutes** **Serves : 4 to 6**

Ingredients

Tomatoes : 450 gms
Coconut : ½ (large)
Green Chillies : 2
Ginger : ½ inch
Sugar : 2 tsp.
Salt to taste
Red Chilli Powder : ¼ tsp.
Water : 2 cups
Chopped Coriander
Ghee, Cumin Seeds,
Asafoetida for Fodni (tadka).

Method

(i) Cook the tomato pieces in 2 cups water. When it cools grind it in a mixer and strain it.
(ii) Extract coconut milk (approximately 1 ½ cups).
(iii) Grind the chillies and ginger.
(iv) Mix together the tomato puree mixture and the coconut milk. To this add salt, sugar, ground chillies and ginger.
(v) Before serving heat ghee, add the cumin seeds, asafoetida and red chilli powder. Pour it over the saar.
(vi) Sprinkle chopped coriander on top.

Vegetable Stew

Preparation Time : 35 minutes **Cooking Time : 10 minutes** **Serves : 6**

Ingredients

Cauliflower : 100 gms (florettes)
Potatoes : 100 gms
Carrots : 100 gms (English)
Peas : 100 gms
Coconut : 1 (medium)
Salt to taste
Tamarind (size of a small beetlenut)
Sugar : ½ tsp.
Oil : 2 tbsp.

Masala to Grind

Poppyseeds : 3 tsp. (roasted)
Grated Dry Coconut : ½ cup, (roasted)
Cloves : 4
Cinnamon : 1 big piece
Black Pepper : 4
Whole Coriander : 1 tbsp. (full)
Red Chilli Powder : ¼ tsp.

Method

(i) Boil and peel potatoes and make pieces.
(ii) Chop the carrots to ¼ inch pieces and boil them. Boil the peas.
(iii) Make florettes (small size) of the cauliflower and boil them.
(iv) Prepare the coconut milk - (thick and thin consistency).
(v) Soak the tamarind in water for some time and squeeze the juce.
(vi) Heat the oil in a skillet. Saute the ground masalas in it.
(vii) Add the vegetables and saute.
(viii) First add the thin coconut milk. Bring to a boil adding salt, tamarind and sugar.
(ix) Add the thick coconut milk and remove from the gas.

Shahi Kofta

Preparation Time : 30 minutes **Cooking time : 30 minutes** **Serves : 4**

Ingredients

Potatoes : 250 gms
Mawa (khoya) : 50 gms
Cottage Cheese (paneer) : 50 gms
Kishmish : 16 pieces
Almonds : 4 (soaked in water)
Castor Sugar : 1 tsp.
Cornflour : 2 tsp.
Salt to taste
Oil to fry

Curry

Onions : 250 gms
Tomatoes : 125 gms
Ginger : 1 inch
Garlic : 6 cloves
Red Chilli Powder : 1 tsp.
Coriander Powder : 1 tbsp.
Cashewnuts : 25 gms
Curds : 1 tbsp.
Malai or Fresh Cream : 1 tbsp.
Garam Masala : 1 tsp.
(Refer method no. : 1)
Turmeric Powder : ¼ tsp.
Salt to taste
Oil : 6 tbsp.

Method (Koftas)

(i) Boil and peel potatoes. Grate and mash them while they are still hot.
(ii) Mash well after adding salt and cornflour.
(iii) Mash the cottage cheese and mawa together. Add castor sugar and mix together.
(iv) Slice the almonds.
(v) Make 8 equal parts of the potato mixture.
(vi) Make 8 equal parts of the paneer-mawa mixture also.
(vii) Flatten out the paneer mawa mixture. Place a few almonds and kishmish in the centre and close the edges to form balls.
(viii) Flatten out the potato mixture. Place the mawa paneer ball in its centre, make a kofta.
(ix) Prepare koftas in this manner and fry till golden brown.

Curry

(i) Cut onion to pieces. Boil and grind to a paste.
(ii) Prepare tomato puree (refer method no. : 3).
(iii) Grind the cashewnuts to a paste. Add little water if necessary.
(iv) Grind the ginger and garlic.
(v) Beat the cream or malai depending on what you use.
(vi) Beat the curds.
(vii) Heat oil in a skillet. Saute the onion paste till brown and oil comes out from the onion.
(viii) Add ginger and garlic and continue to saute.
(ix) Add turmeric and coriander powder. Add the tomato puree and saute.
(x) Remove from gas and add red chilli powder. Place it on the gas again and saute.
(xi) Add the cream and curds and stir.
(xii) Add salt and cashewnut paste and saute. Add water and stir. Bring to boil.
(xiii) Add garam masala.
(xiv) Just before serving, add the koftas in the curry and give two boils. Do not boil it too much.

Dal Dhokli

Preparation Time : 20 minutes **Cooking time : 10 minutes** **Serves : 6**

Ingredients

Toor Dal : ½ cup (100 gms)
Salt to taste
Wheat Flour : 1 cup
Red Chilli Powder : 1 tsp.
Peanuts : ¼ cup (boiled)
Tamarind : size of a beetlenut
Jaggery : a little
Kharik : 6
Whole Coriander Powder : ¼ tsp. }
Cumin Powder : ¼ tsp. } while kneading the wheat flour
Oil : 2 tbsp. }
Turmeric Powder,
Red Chilli Powder,
Salt to taste
Whole Coriander Powder : ½ tsp.
Cumin Powder : ½ tsp.
Salt to taste
Red Chilli Powder : 1 tsp.
Asafoetida and Mustard for Fodni
Turmeric Powder : ¼ tsp.
Cinnamon : 2 inches

Method

(i) Wash and cook toor dal.
(ii) Knead a firm dough by adding the ingredients mentioned above to wheat flour.
(iii) Roll out rotis and cut out pieces in the shape of 'Shankarpalis' (diamond shape).
(iv) Beat the cooked dal.
(v) Heat oil. Add asafoetida, mustard, turmeric and cinnamon, then the dal. Add kharik pieces and the peanuts.
(vi) Add water to get a thinner consistancy of the dal.
(vii) Add red chilli powder, salt, coriander powder and cumin powder.
(viii) When it begins to boil add the dhoklis one by one.
(ix) When the dhoklis are cooked add jaggary and tamarind
(x) Serve by adding ghee on top.

***Important Note :** If you serve this dish with a salad then its as good as a full meal.*

Try this : When you serve lemon juice, try adding some ginger juice to it. This tastes very good and different.

Spring Onion Pulao and Peas Pulao

Punjabi Samosa and Veg Burgers

Masoor Dal (Lentils) Kofta Curry

Preparation Time : 30 minutes **Cooking Time : 30 minutes** **Serves : 6**

Ingredients

Lentils : ½ cup
Coconut : ¼
Onions : 2 (medium)
Red Chilli Powder and
Salt to taste
Oil to fry

Curry

Onions : 3 (medium)
Tomatoes : 2 (medium)
Garlic Cloves : 8
Ginger : ½"
Coriander Powder : 1 tbsp.
Cumin Powder : ½ tsp.
Red Chilli Powder : 1 tsp.
Turmeric Powder : ¼ tsp.
Salt to taste
Garam Masala : ½ tsp.
(Refer method no. : 1)

Garnish

Chopped Coriander

Method (Koftas)

(i) Soak the lentils overnight in water.
(ii) Drain in the collander. Grind coarsely.
(iii) Grate onions and squeeze to remove excess water.
(iv) Grate the coconut.
(v) Mix the lentils, onions, coconut, salt and red chilli powder and make lemon size balls (10-12). Fry them in oil till golden brown.

Curry

(i) Chop onions then grind in a mixer.
(ii) Prepare tomato puree (refer method no. : 3).
(iii) Grind the garlic and ginger.
(iv) Heat 4 tbsp. oil in a vessel. Saute onions till brown. Add the ground ginger and garlic and saute.
(v) Add turmeric powder, coriander powder and cumin powder and saute.
(vi) Remove from gas, add red chilli powder and saute.
(vii) Place on gas and add tomato puree and saute. Add 2 cups water and let it cook. Add salt and garam masala. Add koftas and boil till cooked. Sprinkle chopped coriander.

Important Note : *If the ground dal still retains some water then tie it in a thin muslin cloth and press the water out. If you are in a hurry to cook after step vii; pressure cook for a minute.*

Masoor and Kaju Curry

Preparation Time : 15 minutes **Cooking Time : 15 minutes** **Serves : 6**

Ingredients

Whole Masoor
Lentils : ½ cup (100 gms)
Cashewnuts : 60 gms or
Fresh Cashewnuts : 100 gms
Tamarind : small beetlenut size
Jaggery : size of peanut
Salt to taste
Red Chilli Powder : 1 tsp.
Turmeric Powder : ½ tsp.
Oil : 2 tbsp.

Masala to Grind

Onion : 1 medium, chopped
Grated fresh coconut : ½ cup
Saraswat Masala : 1 tbl sp.
} saute in little oil and grind to a paste

Method

(i) Soak lentils overnight or 6 hours in advance.
(ii) Soak cashewnuts for 1 hour. Remove skin.
(iii) Heat oil. Add red chilli powder and turmeric.
(iv) Add lentils and cashewnuts. Saute well.
(v) Add water and cook.
(vi) When almost done add saraswat masala, sauted and ground onion and coconut paste.
(vii) Add salt, tamarind (soaked and squeezed) and jaggery.
(viii) Let it boil a little.
(ix) Add chopped coriander.

Important Note : *Only saute the onions and coconut in oil. Grind it and add saraswat masala (refer method no. : 1) , 1 tsp. only. If fresh cashewnuts (kaju) are not available then soak the dried ones in water.*

Paneer Potato Kofta Curry

Preparation Time : 30 minutes **Cooking time : 20 minutes** **Serves : 6**

Ingredients

Filling for Koftas

Paneer : 100 gms
Peas : ½ cup (boiled)
Green Chillies : 2
Ginger : ½ inches
Salt to taste
Chopped Coriander

Covering for Koftas

Potatoes : ½ kg
Cornflour : 1 tsp.
Salt to taste
Oil to fry

Curry

Onions : 3 (medium)
Tomatoes : 3 (medium)
Ginger : ½ inches
Coriander Powder : 2 tsp.
Cumin Powder : ½ tsp.
Garam Masala : 1 tsp.
(Refer method no. : 1)
Cream Curds : 1 tbsp.
(Refer glossary)
Red Chilli Powder : 1 tsp.
Turmeric Powder : ¼ tsp.
Salt to taste
Oil : 4 tbsp.

Method (Koftas)

(i) Crush the paneer.
(ii) Chop the ginger and chillies finely.
(iii) Chop the coriander fine.
(iv) Prepare the filling by mixing the paneer, peas, coriander, ginger, green chillies and salt.

Kofta Covering

(i) Boil potatoes and grate when warm.
(ii) Add cornflour and salt and mash till soft.
(iii) Prepare lemon size balls. Flatten each ball and fill with filling and prepare koftas and deep fry till golden brown.

Curry

(i) Chop onions and grind in a mixer.
(ii) Prepare tomato puree (refer method no. : 3).
(iii) Grind the ginger. Beat the curds.
(iv) Heat oil. Saute onion paste till brown and add tomato puree and saute.
(v) Add cumin powder, turmeric powder, coriander powder and ground ginger and saute.
(vi) Remove from gas and add red chilli powder.
(vii) Place on gas, and stir; add curds.
(viii) Add salt and water. Let it cook. Add garam masala.
(ix) Before serving add koftas to the curry and give 2 boils. Garnish with chopped corainder.

Baghdadi Curry

Preparation Time : 40 minutes **Cooking Time : 15 minutes** **Serves : 6**

Ingredients

Small Potatoes : 250 gms
(walnut size)
French Beans : 100 gms
English Carrots : 100 gms
Shelled Peas : ½ cup
Spring Onions : 1 bunch
Coconut Milk : 1 cup
Water : 2 ½ cups
Vanaspati Ghee : 3 tbsp.
Turmeric Powder : ½ tsp.
Worcesterschire Sauce : 1 tbsp.
Almonds : 15
Sultanas : 1 tbsp.
Cream (malai) : 2 tbsp.
Curds : 2 tbsp.
Kashmiri Masala : 1 tsp.
(Refer method no. : 1)
Salt to taste

Masala to Grind

Kashmiri or Reshampatti
Chillies : 6
Ginger : 1 inch
Garlic : 8 cloves
White Sesame Seeds : 2 tsp. full
Poppy Seeds : 2 tsp. full
Cumin : 2 tsp.
Grated Coconut : 6 tbsp.
Red Vinegar : 1 ½ tbsp.

Method

(i) Boil and peel potatoes.
(ii) Cut beans and carrots diamond-shaped.
(iii) Boil beans, carrots and peas (not too soft).
(iv) In little ghee saute the above vegetables and potatoes lightly.
(v) Soak almonds in water. Peel and make slivers and saute in little ghee.
(vi) Saute sultanas in ghee till they swell.
(vii) Beat the cream and curds separately.
(viii) Slice the onions thinly. Do not use the shoots.
(ix) In a flat bowl (not very deep) heat ghee and saute onions till they are soft but translucent.
(x) Add coconut milk and 1 cup water. Add turmeric and ground masala. Saute and cover for 10 to 15 minutes till it cooks.
(xi) Add cream and mix.
(xii) Add curds and stir.
(xiii) Add all the vegetables.
(xiv) Add almonds and sultanas.
(xv) Add salt and mix.
(xvi) Add kashmiri masala, Worcesterschire sauce (This sauce is easily available in the market.) Stir and remove from gas.

Dal Makhani

Preparation Time : 30 to 40 minutes   Cooking Time : 10 minutes   Serves : 6 to 8

Ingredients

Whole Black Beans : 1 cup
Chana Dal : ½ cup
Red Kidney Beans : ¼ cup
Onion : 1 (medium)
Tomatoes : 200 gms
Green chillies : 5 to 6
Ginger : 1 inch (ground)
Oil : 3 tbsp.
Salt to taste
Amul Butter : 1 tbsp.
Whipped Cream : 1 tbsp.
Homemade Thick Ghee : 2 tbsp.
Red Chilli Powder : 1 tsp.

Method

(i) Soak the kidney beans overnight.
(ii) Pick and wash the chana dal and the black beans.
(iii) Pressure Cook the chana dal and black beans together and the kidney beans separately in water. It takes 30-40 minutes.
(iv) When they are cooked, mash.
(v) Chop the onions and tomatoes finely.
(vi) Chop chillies finely lengthwise.
(vii) Heat oil in a vessel. Saute the chillies and onions well.
(viii) Add ground ginger and saute.
(ix) Add tomatoes and saute.
(x) Add the blended mixture of chana dal and black beans and the kidney beans. See that the consistency remains thickish.
(xi) Add salt and bring to boil.
(xii) Add whipped cream and mix well.
(xiii) Add the Amul butter.
(xiv) Heat some ghee. Remove from the gas when hot and add red chilli powder. Pour this on dal.

Important Note : *Soak tomatoes in hot water. Then peel skins and chop finely. This way the skins can be avoided.*

Kadhi Pakoda

Preparation Time : 25 minutes **Cooking time : 20 minutes** **Serves : 4 to 6**

Ingredients

Thick Buttermilk : 4 cups
Gram Flour (besan) : 1 tbsp.
Fenugreek Seeds : ¼ tsp.
Asafoetida : ¼ tsp.
Turmeric Powder : ¼ tsp.
Salt to taste
Cloves : 2
Oil or Melted Ghee : 2 tbsp.

Pakodas

Gram (besan) : 1 cup
Onion : 1 (small)
Green Chillies : 3
Salt to taste
Soda Bicarb : $^1/_8$ tsp.
Handful of Chopped Coriander

For Fodni (tadka)

Ghee : 1 tbsp. (homemade)
Red Chilli Powder : 1 tsp.

Method

(i) Add gram flour to the buttermilk and mix well. Add salt and turmeric powder.
(ii) In oil or ghee prepare tadka with fenugreek seeds and asafoetida and add it to the buttermilk.
(iii) Place on heat till the buttermilk rises.

Pakodas

(i) Chop onions and chillies fine.
(ii) Add onions, chillies, coriander, salt and little turmeric to gram flour and mix well.
(iii) Add water and mix well (like cake mixture consistency).
(iv) Add Soda Bicarb before preparing pakodas and whip it a little.
(v) Deep fry pakodas in oil. Add to the kadhi and let it cook a little.
(vi) Heat ghee. Add red chilli powder to it. Pour this on the kadhi before serving.

Important Note : *Prepare thick buttermilk from curds.*

Raw Banana Kofta Curry

Preparation Time : 30 minutes **Cooking Time : 20 minutes** **25 Koftas**

Ingredients

Raw Bananas : 6
(triangular shaped - teen dhari)
Alu Bukhara : 25 (dried)
Soda Bicarb : ¼ tsp.
Red Chilli Powder : ½ tsp.
Turmeric Powder : ¼ tsp.
Coriander Powder : 1 tsp.
Garam Masala : ½ tsp.
(refer method no. : 1)
Gram Flour : 4 tbsp. (full)
Salt to taste
Oil to fry

Curry

Onions : 2 (big)
Tomatoes : 2 (big), pureed
(Refer method no. : 3)
Green Chillies : 4
Garlic Cloves : 8 to 10
Ginger : 1 inch
Coriander Powder : 2 tsp.
Red Chilli Powder : 1 tsp.
Garam Masala : 1 tsp.
(Refer method no. : 1)
Salt to taste
Oil : 6 tbsp.
Water : 4 to 5 cups
Chopped Coriander

Method (Koftas)

(i) Cut bananas with skins, into two pieces, widthwise.
(ii) Cook in the pressure cooker. Do not add water.
(iii) Peel when it is hot, mash it to a soft pulp.
(iv) Add soda, gram flour, salt and remaining masala and knead well. If required add water.
(v) While preparing each kofta, put alu bukhara in the centre.
(vi) Fry till deep brown in oil.

Curry

(i) Grate onions or grind in the mixer.
(ii) Chop the garlic, ginger and chillies fine or grind the ginger and garlic in mixer.
(iii) Heat oil. Add cumin, ginger, garlic, chillies and onions and saute till golden brown. Add coriander powder and turmeric and saute. Remove from heat. Add red chilli powder. Saute and place on gas. Add tomato puree and saute well. Add water and boil. Add salt. Boil. Add koftas and boil. Add garam masala and chopped coriander.

Important Note : *This curry tastes very good because of the Alubukhara.*

Dhansak

Preparation Time : 30 minutes **Cooking Time : 15 minutes** **Serves : 4 to 6**

Ingredients

Toor Dal : 2 tbsp.
Masoor Dal : 2 tbsp.
Moong Dal : 2 tbsp.
Gram Dal : 2 tbsp.
White Split Beans : 1 tbsp.
Onion : 1 (medium)
Tomato : 1 (medium)
Brinjal : 1 (small)
Potatoes : 2 (medium)
Sweet Potato : 1 (small)
Red Pumpkin : 25 gms
Methi or Fenugreek : 6 bunches (small size)
Mint Sprigs : 6 (only leaves)
Coriander : a handful
Green Chillies : 2
Coriander and Cumin Powder : ½ tsp.
Turmeric Powder : ½ tsp. each
Ground Pepper : ½ tsp.
Dhansak Masala : 1 tsp. (available in the market)
Salt to taste

Masala to Grind

Ginger : 1 inch
Garlic : 6 cloves

Masala to Roast and to Grind

Dry Coconut : 1" to 1 ½" (grated)
Cumin Seeds : ½ tsp.
Red Chilli Powder : ½ tsp.

For Fodni (tadka)

Onion : 1 (small)
Tomato : 1 (small)
Oil : 2 tbsp.

Method

(i) Pick and wash all the dals well.
(ii) All ingredients from onions to green chillies should be chopped.
(iii) Leaving the dhansak masala and the fodni (tadka) ingredients, the remaining ingredients and dals and chopped vegetables should be cooked in the pressure cooker with enough water.
(iv) Press the cooked material through a soup strainer.
(v) Chop onion and tomato finely.
(vi) Heat oil and saute onion till brownish.
(vii) Add tomato and saute.
(viii) Add the dal mixture. Add salt, dhansak masala and give 4 to 6 boils.
(ix) Serve the Parsi pulav alongwith dhansak.

Special Sambar

Preparation Time : 25 minutes **Cooking Time : 15 minutes** **Serves : 6 to 8**

Ingredients

Fresh Coconut : 1 (big)
Cornflour : 2 tsp. (almost full)
Green Chillies : 10 to 12
Peanuts Powder : 2 tbsp.
Tamarind : the size of beetlenut
Salt to taste
Sugar : 1 tsp.
Curry Leaves : 8 to 9
Oil : 2 to 3 tbsp.
Mustard and Asafoetida for Fodni

Masala to Grind

(add water)
Coriander : 2 tbsp.
Turmeric powder : ½ tsp.

For Garnish

Chopped Coriander

Method

(i) Extract thick and thin milk from coconut. Mix together and add cornflour.
(ii) Slice the chillies in the centre halfway.
(iii) Soak the tamarind in the water and squeeze to make a pulp.
(iv) Chop curry leaves coarsely.
(v) Heat oil in a vessel and prepare fodni (tadka) and add chillies.
(vi) When the chillies are well-fried sprinkle peanut powder and saute. Add masala and saute.
(vii) Stir the coconut milk and add it.
(viii) Add salt, sugar, tamarind pulp and curry leaves and boil a bit. This allows the cornflour to cook and the sambar gets the aroma of chillies.
(ix) This sambar is not too thin or too thick.
(x) Garnish with chopped coriander.

Important Note : *This sambar tastes delicious. As coconuts, chillies and other ingredients are easily available in each house this tasty and special curry can be prepared when you face a 'last minute' crisis.*

Nawabi Curry

Preparation Time : 15 minutes **Cooking Time : 30 minutes** **Serves : 4 to 6**

Ingredients

Potatoes : 12 (very small)
Pearl Onions : 12
Carrots : 100 gms
Yam : 200 gms
Pineapple : 3 slices
Cherries : 12 (fresh or tinned)
Capsicum : 1 (big)
Toothpicks : 12 (6" size)
Oil for frying

Curry

Onions : 200 gms
Tomatoes : 125 gms
Curds : ¼ cup
Cream (malai) : ¼ cup
Coriander Powder : 1 tbsp.
Cumin Seed Powder : ½ tsp.
Turmeric : ½ tsp.
Red Chilli Powder : 1 tsp.
Pinch of Sugar
Garlic Cloves : 8 to 10 } grind
Ginger : 1" inch }
Almonds : 6
Poppy Seeds : 3 tsp. (grind)
Oil : ¼ cup
Salt to taste

Method

(i) Peel the potatoes and onions and parboil them.
(ii) Boil the yam and slice into ½, ½" and ¼" thick pieces.
(iii) Deep fry the potatoes and yam till golden brown.
(iv) Slice carrots into pieces bigger than ¼" and boil.
(v) Slice pineapple into ½" pieces and press to remove water.
(vi) Cut capsicum to 12 pieces and boil till it changes colour.
(vii) On each toothpick insert all vegetables from potatoes to capsicum (one piece of each) and keep aside.

Curry

(i) Grate the onions.
(ii) Prepare tomato puree (refer method no. : 3).
(iii) Soak the almonds in water. Then peel them.
(iv) Grind the peeled almonds and poppy seeds to a paste.
(v) Beat the curds and cream.
(vi) Saute onions in oil till brownish. Add ground garlic and ginger and saute. Add cumin and coriander powder and saute. Add turmeric powder.
(vii) Remove from gas and add red chilli powder and saute. Place on the heat. Add the almond and poppy seeds paste and saute. Add tomato puree and saute. Add little water and let it cook.
(viii) Add the beaten cream and curds and then the salt.
(ix) Boil the curry well. Whilst boiling add the toothpicks. Stir gently. Switch off the gas after some time.
(x) Before serving remove the toothpicks and pour curry into a deep oval shape bowl and add the toothpicks.
(xi) Sprinkle chopped corainder on top.

Important Note : *If the toothpick size does not match the above mentioned one then you can use thin rods of that size of steel or any other material.*

Paneer Peas Curry

Preparation Time : 15 minutes **Cooking Time : 30 minutes** **Serves : 4 to 6**

Ingredients

Paneer (cottage cheese) : 150 gms
Shelled Peas : 1 ½ cups
Onions : 2 large (200 gms)
Tomato : 1 large (125 gms)
Garlic Cloves : 6 } To
Ginger : 1 inch } (grind)
Red Chilli Powder : 1 tsp.
Turmeric : ½ tsp.
Coriander Powder : 2 tsp.
Cumin Powder : ½ tsp.
Garam Masala : ½ tsp.
(Refer method no. : 1)
Curds : 2 tbsp.
Cream (malai) : 1 tbsp.
Poppy Seeds : 3 tsp.
Salt to taste
Oil : 6 tbsp.
Bay Leaves : 2

For Garnish

Chopped Coriander

Method

(i) Slice cottage cheese into ½" × ½" and ¼" thick pieces. Deep fry till golden brown and place in hot water.
(ii) Boil the shelled peas and keep aside.
(iii) Grate the onions.
(iv) Prepare tomato puree (refer method no. : 3).
(v) Add a little water to poppy seeds and grind to a paste.
(vi) Beat the curds and cream together.
(vii) Heat oil in a vessel. Add bay leaves and grated onions and saute. When the onion turns yellowish, remove the bay leaves and saute till the onions are brownish.
(viii) Add ground garlic and ginger. Saute and add turmeric. Add coriander and cumin powder and saute.
(ix) Remove from gas. Add red chilli powder, stir and place on the gas.
(x) Add ground poppy seeds and saute.
(xi) Add tomato puree. Pour a little water and let it cook.
(xii) Add beaten curds and salt.
(xiii) Add peas and cottage cheese and let it boil a bit. Add garam masala. Sprinkle chopped coriander.

Shahi Cauliflower

Preparation Time : 10 minutes **Cooking Time : 20 minutes** **Serves : 4**

Ingredients

Cauliflower : 250 gms
Milk : 1 cup
Cream (malai) : 2 tbsp.
Oil : 1 tbsp.
Cumin : ½ tsp.
Cinnamon Powder : ¼ tsp.
Cumin Powder : ½ tsp.
Salt and Green Chillies Paste to taste
Oil or Ghee to fry

Method

(i) Cut the flower to medium florettes. Slice off skin of the stalks (for speedy cooking).
(ii) Fry them in oil or ghee. Don't let the colour change too much.
(iii) Beat the cream (malai).
(iv) Heat the oil. Add cumin and green chilli paste.
(v) After sauteing a bit add the florettes. Saute a little. Add the milk. When almost cooked add cream, salt and both the powders. There should be some gravy in this dish.

Quick and Easy Vegetable

Preparation Time : 10 minutes **Cooking Time : 10 minutes** **Serves : 4 to 6**

Ingredients

Dried White Peas : 250 gms
Onions : 2 (medium)
ginger : ½ inch make a
Garlic Cloves : 6 paste
Saraswat Masala : 1 tsp.
(Refer method no. : 1)
Salt to taste
Oil : 3 tbsp.
Chopped Coriander

Method

(i) Soak the peas overnight.
(ii) Chop the onions fine.
(iii) Cook the peas in a pressure cooker (when the whistle sounds, keep for 15 minutes on low flame).
(iv) Remove water from the cooked peas and keep aside.
(v) Heat oil in a vessel. Saute onions till golden brown and add ginger and garlic paste and saute.
(vi) Add peas and saute. Add very little water from the cooked peas, salt and the masala. Let it cook. If required add some more water.
(vii) This curry should have gravy. Sprinkle chopped coriander.

Shahi Gobhi (Cabbage)

Preparation Time : 10 minutes **Cooking Time : 15 minutes** **Serves : 3 to 4**

Ingredients

Cabbage : 300 gms
Cottage cheese
(paneer) : 100 gms.
(Refer method no. : 6)
Green Chillies : 1 to 2
Lemon Juice : 1 tsp.
Salt to taste
Pinch of Pepper
Oil : 2 tbsp.
Cumin Seeds : 1/8 tsp.
Mustard : 1/8 tsp.
Pinch of Turmeric Powder

Method

(i) Slice cabbage fine.
(ii) Cut chillies lengthwise.
(iii) Knead the cottage cheese well and add salt and pepper for taste.
(iv) Heat oil in a vessel. Add mustard, cumin, asafoetida, turmeric powder and chillies.
(v) Add the sliced cabbage and saute, cover and cook. See that it does not become too soft. Add the salt. Crush the cottage cheese lightly add and mix. Add pepper and stir lightly. Remove from heat immediately. Add lemon juice.

Important Note : *This vegetable dish is not only tasty but full of proteins.*

Jack fruit Ceylonese Style

Preparation Time : 40 minutes **Cooking Time : 15 minutes** **Serves : 8**

Ingredients

Tender Raw Jackfruit : 1 kilo
Green Chillies : 4
Kokam : 6
Garlic Cloves : 6
Ginger : 1 inch
Onions : 2 (medium)
Curry Leaves : 10 to 12
Red Chilli Powder : ½ tsp.
Coconut : 1 (medium)
Madrasi Onions : 250 gms (shallots)
Oil : 4 tbsp.
Turmeric : ¼ tsp.
Salt to taste,
Lemon Juice : 2 tsp.
Homemade Ghee - 1 tbsp.

Masalas to Grind

Fresh Grated Coconut : 2 tbsp. full
Coriander : 1 tsp.
Cumin Seeds : 1 tsp.
Mustard : 1 tsp.
} roast a little
Rice : 1 tbsp.
Madrasi Onions : 8 to 10 (shallots)

Masala to be roasted and pound finely

Coriander : 3 tbsp.
Cumin : 1 ½ tbsp.
Fennel Seeds : 1 tbsp.
Cinnamon : 2 inches piece
Curry Leaves : 6

Method

(i) Peel the jackfruit and remove the central stalk. Cut ½" to ¾" pieces of the remaining fruit and soak in water.
(ii) Prepare thick, thin and medium : 3 types of milk from the coconut.
(iii) Slice onions.
(iv) Slice the Madrasi onions.
(v) Cut the chillies lengthwise.
(vi) Chop the ginger and garlic fine.
(vii) Roast the red chilli powder a little.
(viii) In the pressure cooker, cook the jackfruit along with onions (not Madrasi), curry leaves, turmeric, garlic, ginger, chillies, kokam, salt and ground masala and thin coconut milk. Cook all this for ½ to ¾ of an hour.
(ix) Add medium coconut milk and cook for ½ to ¾ hr. By this time the jackfruit should have become soft. If it's not soft, then cook it again.
(x) Heat oil. Add Madrasi onions and saute till golden brown. Add the pounded masala and saute. Add the thick milk and the cooked jackfruit and let it boil. Add red chilly powder. Add lemon juice and salt (if needed).
(xi) Before serving prepare a fodni (tadka) of red chilly powder and homemade ghee and pour on top.

French Beans Madrasi Style

Preparation Time : 15 minutes **Cooking Time : 10 minutes** **Serves : 3 to 4**

Ingredients

French Beans : 250 gms
Pinch of Soda
Lemon Juice : 1 tsp.
Salt to taste
Oil : 1 tbsp.
Mustard for Fodni (tadka)

Masalas to Grind

Fresh Grated Coconut : ¼ cup
Madrasi Onions : 4 to 6
Green Chillies : 1 to 2
Curry Leaves : 6 (small)
Black Pepper : 4 to 5

Method

(i) Chop beans into ½" width pieces.
(ii) Add a pinch of soda to water and boil the beans in it. Do not cook them too soft. Drain water.
(iii) Heat oil in a vessel and add mustard. When it begins to splutter add ground masala and saute.
(iv) Add french beans, lemon juice and salt and mix. Remove from gas after sometime.

Important Note : *This vegetable tastes different from the routine one and delicious too.*

Raw Tomato Curry

Preparation Time : 10 minutes **Cooking Time : 20 minutes** **Serves : 4**

Ingredients

Green Raw Tomatoes : 300 gms
Onion : 1 (medium)
Green Chillies : 2
Coriander Powder : 1 tbsp.
Red Chilli Powder : ¼ tsp.
Salt and Sugar to taste
Coconut Milk : 1 cup (thick)
Mustard, Asafoetida, Turmeric Powders for Fodni (tadka)
Oil : 2 tbsp.
Handful of Chopped Coriander

Method

(i) Chop the tomatoes into big pieces.
(ii) Slice onions.
(iii) Slice the chillies lengthwise.
(iv) Heat oil in a vessel. Prepare the fodni (tadka).
(v) Add chillies and onions, saute till translucent.
(vi) Add coriander powder and red chilli powder. Then add tomatoes, cover and cook.
(vii) Pour the coconut milk, salt and sugar.
(viii) Give 2 to 3 boils.
(ix) Add chopped coriander.

Cauliflower Masala Moghlai

Preparation Time : 30 minutes **Cooking Time : 15 minutes** **Serves : 4 people**

Ingredients

Cauliflower : 500 gms
French Beans : 100 gms
Onions : 250 gms
Tomatoes : 250 gms
Cream Curds : 2 tbsp.
Coriander Powder : 1 tsp.
Cumin Powder : 1 tsp.
Red Chilli Powder : ½ tsp.
Turmeric Powder : ¼ tsp.
Garam Masala : ½ tsp.
(Refer method no. : 1)
Vanaspati Ghee : 3 tbsp. (level)
Chopped Coriander
Garlic Cloves : 4 }
Ginger : ½ inch } grind
Green Chillies : 2 }

Method

(i) Make medium florettes. Skin the stalks.
(ii) Chop the french beans fine.
(iii) Place tomatoes in hot water. Peel and chop them.
(iv) Grind the onions in a mixer.
(v) Beat the full cream curds well.
(vi) Heat ghee in a pressure cooker. Saute onions till golden brown.
(vii) Add ground masala and saute.
(viii) Add tomato, cream curds and salt. Saute till the oil begins to leave the mixture.
(ix) Add florettes and masalas except chopped coriander and garam masala powder and saute. Add a little water and cook in the pressure cooker.
(x) When the whistle sounds reduce flame and cook it for 3 minutes.
(xi) Remove from heat and when the pressure drops, open the cover. Add garam masala and stir lightly.
(xii) Transfer to a serving bowl and sprinkle chopped coriander.

Dahi Rajma (Kidney Beans in Curds)

Preparation Time : 10 minutes **Cooking Time : 1 hours** **Serves : 4 to 6**

Ingredients

Red Kidney Beans : 1 cup
Curds : 1 cup (not from fridge)
Full Cream Curds : ½ cup
Cornflour : 1 tsp.
Green Chillies : 2
Ginger : 1" (ground)
Coriander Powder : 1 ½ tbsp.
Chopped Coriander : ¼ cup
Salt to taste
Thick Ghee (homemade) : 1 tbsp.
Red Chilli Powder : 1 tsp.

Method

(i) Soak the red kidney beans overnight.
(ii) The next day cook it in a pressure cooker till soft (this would take ½ to ¾ of an hour).
(iii) Beat both the curds well and add cornflour and mix well.
(iv) Slice chillies vertically into thin slices.
(v) Heat oil in a vessel, add chillies and ground ginger and saute. Add coriander powder and saute. Add the beaten curds and continue to saute continuously.
(vi) Add salt and stir.
(vii) Remove the water from the beans and keep aside. Add beans to the curds and cook till thick. Add chopped coriander.
(viii) Heat ghee and add red chilli powder. Pour this over the beans just before serving on the table.

Important Note : *If you do not soak the beans overnight you can directly pressure cook it. But it requires about 1 hour to cook well. First cook the beans in the cooker. After the whistle sounds reduce flame and cook for ½ hr. When the pressure drops stir the beans well and again pressure cook for ½ hr.*

Paneer Korma (Type 1)

Preparation Time : 15 to 20 minutes Cooking Time : 30 minutes Serves : 6

Ingredients

Paneer (cottage cheese) : 250 gms (not homemade)
Onions : 250 gms
Tomatoes : 125 gms (pureed)
Green Chillies : 1
Turmeric Powder : 1/8 tsp.
Red Chilli Powder : ½ tsp.
Sugar : 1 tsp.
Salt to taste
Cashewnuts : 8
Curds : 1 tbsp.
Thick Cream (malai) : 1 tbsp.
Little Chopped Coriander
Oil : 6 tbsp.

Masala to Grind

Garlic : 6 cloves
Ginger : ½ inch
Green chillies : 2

For Garnish

Garam Masala : 1/4 tsp.

Method

(i) Cut the cottage cheese into pieces, a little less thick than ¼" and 1 ¼". Soak them in hot water.
(ii) Chop onions and boil the pieces in water. Remove water and grind to a paste in a mixer.
(iii) Soak cashewnuts in little water. When soft grind to a paste in a mixer.
(iv) Beat the curds and cream separately and keep aside.
(v) Chop the chillies fine.
(vi) Prepare tomato puree (refer method no. : 3).
(vii) Take 2 to 3 tbsp. from the puree. Boil it alongwith a little oil, salt and little sugar. Keep aside.
(viii) Heat oil and saute onions till golden brown. Add bayleaf, cardamom and cinnamon pieces.
(ix) Add ½ cup water & boil. Add sugar and salt.
(x) Add beaten curds and turmeric powder and stir.
(xi) Add ground masala and saute.
(xii) Add the tomato puree which was not boiled. Add red chilli powder.
(xiii) Add cashew paste. Mix and add the beaten cream (malai).
(xiv) In another vessel heat 1 tbsp. oil. Add the boiled puree and saute. Add chillies, coriander, a little sugar and salt and saute.
(xv) Remove the paneer from the water and keep aside. Add paneer. Add the ready gravy on this. Let it boil a bit and sprinkle garam masala and mix.

Tawa Paneer, Shahi Kofta and Naan

Cream of Tomato Soup

Paneer Korma (Type 2)

Preparation Time : 15 minutes **Cooking Time : 15 to 20 minutes** **Serves : 4 to 6**

Ingredients

Paneer (cottage cheese) : 250 gms
Oil to fry
Water : 1 cup
Salt : ¼ tsp.
Garam Masala : ½ tsp.
(Refer method no. : 1)
Onion : 1 (medium)
Green Chillies : 3
Ginger : ½ inch
Oil : 1 tbsp.
Butter : 1 tbsp.
Flour : 1 ½ tbsp.
Milk : 1 cup
Water : 1 cup
Boiled Peas : ½ cup (optional)
Salt to taste
Chopped Coriander
Cumin Seeds : ¼ tsp.
Red Chilli powder : ½ tsp.
Thick Ghee : 1 tsp. (homemade)

Method

(i) Cut cottage cheese into quarter inch thick and ½ or ¾ inch pieces.
(ii) Add salt and garam masala to 1 cup water stir and keep aside.
(iii) Deep fry cottage cheese pieces till golden brown. Soak them in the above mentioned water and boil them till soft. Turn off the gas and let the cottage cheese remain in the water.
(iv) Chop the onions, chillies and ginger fine.
(v) Mix the water and milk together. Heat and keep aside.
(vi) Heat oil and butter and saute onions till they are golden brown. Add chillies and ginger and saute.
(vii) Add flour and mix together. Add the hot water milk mixture gradually, continue to stir so that no lumps are formed. When the entire milk is poured, add the cottage cheese and the masala water. If required add salt. Boil till the gravy is thick. Add peas (optional).
(viii) Before serving, prepare fodni with heated ghee, cumin seeds and red chilli powder. Pour this over the ready cottage cheese gravy and garnish with chopped coriander.

Bhindi Rassewali

Preparation Time : 10 minutes **Cooking Time : 15 minutes** **Serves : 4**

Ingredients

Bhindi : 250 gms
Onion : 1 (medium)
Fresh Chopped Mint : 1 tbsp.
Tamarind : small beetlenut size
Salt to taste

Masalas to Grind

Garlic : 8 cloves
Kashmiri Red Chillies : 4

Method

(i) Wipe the bhindis with a wet cloth. Cut each one into 1 inch pieces.
(ii) Chop the onions fine.
(iii) Soak the tamarind in water. When it softens prepare a pulp.
(iv) Heat 2 tbsp. oil in a vessel and saute onions. Add the ground masala and saute. Add a little water and allow the ground masala to cook well.
(v) Add bhindi and some salt immediately. Let it cook.
(vi) Now add tamarind pulp. Let this cook for sometime.
(vii) Now add the finely chopped mint leaves. Mix well.

Cauliflower Potato Punjabi Style

Preparation Time : 15 minutes **Cooking Time : 20 minutes** **Serves : 4**

Ingredients

Cauliflower Florettes : 400 gms
Potatoes : 200 gms
Green Chillies : 2
Ginger : 1 inch
Coriander Powder : 1 ½ tbsp.
Thick Ghee (homemade) : 1 tbl sp (level)
Red Chilli Powder : 1 tsp. (level)
Chopped Coriander
Oil : 2 tbsp.
Cumin Seeds : ¼ tsp.
Pinch of Asafoetida
Salt and Dried Mango Powder (aamchur) to taste

Method

(i) Make big size florettes from the cauliflowers.
(ii) Peel potatoes and chop them into long big pieces.
(iii) Slice chillies vertically.
(iv) Chop the ginger fine.
(v) Heat oil in a vessel. Add cumin, asafoetida, chillies and ginger and saute.
(vi) Add coriander powder and salt. Add the florettes and potatoes and saute.
(vii) Transfer this to a pressure cooker alongwith ¼ cup water and cook for 2 to 3 minutes.
(viii) Heat ghee in a vessel. Add red chilli powder and the above mixture. Stir after adding the dry mango powder. This dish not only requires less time but tastes different from other cauliflower dishes commonly prepared.

Bhindi in Coconut Milk

Preparation Time : 25 minutes **Cooking Time : 15 minutes** **Serves : 4**

Ingredients

Bhindi (okra)* : 20 (long variety)
Coconut Milk : thick and thin of ½ coconut
Fresh Grated Coconut : ½ cup
Salt and Red Chilli Powder to taste
Kala Masala : ½ tsp.
(Refer method no. : 1)
Oil : 2 to 3 tbsp.

Masalas to be roasted lightly and ground

Sesame Seeds : 1 tbsp. (white)
Poppy Seeds : 1 tbsp.
Coriander Seeds : 1 tbsp.
Tamarind : a little (not to be roasted)

Method

(i) Wipe the bhindis with a damp cloth, cut into 2 inch pieces and give lengthwise a cut in the centre (do not divide in two pieces).
(ii) Saute the grated coconut over a little oil till golden brown, grind it coarsely.
(iii) Mix the ground masala and the ground coconut well. Add red chilli powder, salt and kala masala. Mix well.
(iv) Stuff above mixture in the bhindi.
(v) Heat oil in a vessel. Add the bhindi and little salt (this prevents the bhindi from becoming sticky).
(vi) Cover the vessel when the bhindi begins to become soft, add the thin coconut milk and let it cook.
(vii) Add the thick milk. Give 2 boils. Remove from the gas.

Important Note : ** This particular variety of bhindi is only available in the rainy season and it is very light green in colour. It is called sat dhari bhindi.*

Aloo Methi (Potato and Fenugreek)

Preparation Time : 20 minutes **Cooking Time : 20 minutes** **Serves : 4**

Ingredients

Fenugreek* : 25 bunches
(small variety)
Onion : 1 (large)
Potatoes : 3 (medium)
Fresh Grated Coconut : ¼ cup
Salt to taste
Red Chilli Powder to taste
Oil : 3 tbsp.

Method

(i) Remove the roots from the fenugreek and wash throughly.
(ii) Dip the bunches 2 to 3 times in water. Clean and remove all the mud and dirt and spread on a cloth to dry.
(iii) Chop them finely and add salt mix and keep aside.
(iv) Boil and peel potatoes. Cut big pieces and keep aside.
(v) Squeeze excess water from fenugreek and keep aside.
(vi) Chop the onions fine.
(vii) Heat oil in a vessel. Add turmeric and onion and saute. Add salt and red chilli powder and saute.
(viii) Add the chopped fenugreek, cover and cook. Add coconut.
(ix) When it cooks well, add the boiled potatoes and mix well. Cover and cook for sometime. Now remove the cover and saute.

Important Note : *This variety of fenugreek is cultivated in sand.*

Kale Chane

Preparation Time : 40 minutes **Cooking Time : 15 minutes** **Serves : 8**

Ingredients

Kabuli Chana
(white chick peas) : 500 gms
Water : 4 cups
Salt : 1 tsp.
Soda Bicarb : ½ tsp.
Tea Powder : 2 tsp. (Hotel Dust)

Masala

Cardamoms : 3 (big)
Green Cardamoms : 6
Dried Pomergranate Seeds : 4 tsp.
Black Pepper : 10
Bay Leaves : 3
Cumin : 2 tsp.
Cinnamon : 1 big piece
Cloves : 4
Black Salt : 1 tsp.

For Fodni (tadka)

Oil : 4 tsp.
Green Chillies : 6
Ginger : 1 big 2 inch piece

Fodni to pour (chok)

Thick Ghee (homemade) : 2 tbsp.
Red Chilli Powder : 2 tsp.

Method

(i) Soak the grams overnight in water.
(ii) Remove the water in the morning.
(iii) Add 4 cups water, salt and soda bicarb. Put the tea powder in a small thin cloth and tie the ends (tea bouquet garni). Dip this in the above and cook the grams in the pressure cooker till soft (for 45 minutes).
(iv) When it is cooked remove the tea bouquet garni.
(v) Remove the water from the cooked grams and keep aside.
(vi) Roast the masalas (except salt) without oil till light brown.
(vii) Add a little water to the masalas and grind it nicely. Add ½ cup water and strain this and repeat this step 2 to 3 times.
(viii) The residue of the strained mixture (solid) should be discarded. To the masala water add black salt.
(ix) Slice the chillies and ginger fine vertically.
(x) Heat oil in a vessel. Add ginger and chillies and saute. Add the masala water and let it boil till the mixture thickens.
(xi) Add the grams to the masala. Add the (kept aside) water, as required. It should not be too watery.
(xii) Taste it and add salt if required.
(xiii) Before serving, heat ghee, add red chilli powder and pour on the grams.
(xiv) Stir and serve it.

Chole (Type 1)

Preparation Time : 30 minutes **Cooking Time : 30 minutes** **Serves : 8**

Ingredients

Chole
(white chick peas) : 500 gms
Soda Bicarb : ½ tsp.
Cumin : ½ tsp.
Black Peppercorns : 6
Bay Leaves : 2
Cardamoms : 2
For Curry
Onions : 4 (large)
Tomatoes : 2 (large)
Red Chilli Powder : 2 tsp.
Salt to Taste
Turmeric Powder : ½ tsp.
Coriander Powder : 3 tbsp.
Pepper Powder : ¼ tsp.
Cinnamon Powder : ¼ tsp.
Cumin Powder : 1 tsp.
Lemon Juice : 01 ½ Lemon
Thick Vanaspati : 2 tbsp.
Garam Masala : ½ tsp.

Masalas to Grind

Garlic : 8 to 10 cloves
Ginger : 1 ½ inch

For Garnish

Chopped Coriander

Method

(i) Pick and wash the chole well and soak overnight in water to which soda bicarb is added.
(ii) Cook the following day in the same water in a pressure cooker after adding all the masala (for ½ an hr.) till soft. Strain and keep the water aside.

Gravy

(i) Chop onions fine or grate them.
(ii) Make tomato puree (refer method no. : 3).
(iii) Heat ghee in a vessel and saute onions till brown.
(iv) Add ginger and garlic paste and saute.
(v) Add coriander powder, cumin powder and saute.
(vi) Add turmeric, red chilli powder and saute.
(vii) Add little water and cook.
(viii) Add tomato puree and cook.
(ix) Add salt, cinnamon and pepper powder.
(x) Add chole gradually and continue stirring.
(xi) Add water from the chole as required and mix well.
(xii) Add lemon juice and garam masala.
(xiii) Sprinkle chopped coriander on top.

***Important Note :** The chole should have some gravy. It should not be too thin.*

Chole (Type 2)

Preparation Time : 40 minutes **Cooking Time : 30 minutes** **Serves : 8**

Ingredients

Chole (white chick peas) : 500 gms
Soda : ½ tsp.
Tea Powder : 2 tsp. (Hotel Dust)
Oil : 3 tbsp.
Salt to taste
Thick Ghee (homemade) : 2 tbsp.
Tomatoes : 2 (medium)
Onion : 1 (medium)
Potatoes : 3 (medium)
Tamarind : Lemon size

Masalas to Grind

Onions : 5 (medium)
Black Pepper : 1 tbsp.
Cumin : 1 tbsp.

For Garnish

Chopped Coriander

Method

(i) Soak the choles in water overnight.
(ii) Cook it in the pressure cooker the following day.
(iii) While cooking add soda and tea powder tied in a thin cloth (bouquet garni) in the chole.
(iv) Soak tamarind in water and make a pulp.
(v) Peel potatoes, cut chips and deep fry.
(vi) Cut thin, round slices of onion and tomatoes.
(vii) The 5 onions for the masala should be cut and placed on the gas with an iron net below it and roast till black. Add cumin and pepper and grind this to a paste.
(viii) Heat oil in a vessel and saute the above masalas. Add a little water, saute.
(ix) Add the tamarind pulp and saute, add chole and saute (remove the bouquet garni). Add salt.
(x) In an oven-proof dish spread half the choles, spread fried potato chips. Spread the remaining choles and arrange the tomato and onion slices. Sprinkle coriander. Melt ghee and pour evenly on all sides and bake in the oven for 10 minutes.

Paneer Bhurji

Preparation Time : 15 minutes **Cooking Time : 15 minutes** **Serves : 4**

Ingredients

Paneer
(cottage cheese) : of 1 lit milk
(Refer method no. : 7)
Onions : 2 (large)
Tomato : 1 (large)
Green Chillies : 2
Coriander Powder : 1 tsp. full
Garam Masala : ½ tsp.
(Refer method no. : 1)
Red Chilli Powder : 1 tsp.
Chopped Coriander : a handful
Salt to taste and pinch
of Turmeric Powder
Oil : 4 tbsp.
Amul Butter : 1 tsp. full

To Grind

Garlic Cloves : 8
Ginger : ½ to ¾ inch

Method

(i) When the paneer is still warm crush it with your hands.
(ii) Chop the onions fine.
(iii) Soak tomatoes in hot water. Peel and chop to small pieces.
(iv) Chop the chillies fine.
(v) Heat oil and saute onions till golden brown.
(vi) Add the ground garlic and ginger and saute.
(vii) Add the chopped chillies and coriander powder and saute.
(viii) Add turmeric powder. Remove from gas, add red chilli powder. Stir and place on gas.
(ix) Add tomatoes and saute.
(x) Add crushed paneer and saute.
(xi) Add the paneer water (½ cup). Let it bubble.
(xii) Add salt, chopped coriander and garam masala. Stir a little and add butter. When it melts remove from gas.

Cauliflower and Tomato Vegetable

Preparation Time : 15 minutes **Cooking Time : 20 minutes** **Serves : 4**

Ingredients

Cauliflower : 500 gms
Tomatoes : 100 gms
Cashewnuts : 50 gms
Green Chillies : 2 (ground)
Ginger : ½ inch (ground)
Salt to taste
Sugar to taste
Cumin : ½ tsp.
Oil : 2 tbsp.

Method

(i) Cut cauliflower to big florettes.
(ii) Peel the stalks and wash well.
(iii) Chop the tomatoes to medium fine pieces.
(iv) If you are using broken cashewnuts then leave them as they are. But if whole cashewnuts are used then split them in the centre to make 2 pieces.
(v) Heat oil in a vessel. Add cumin seeds.
(vi) Add florettes and cashewnuts. Toss them. Cover it with plate and pour some water on the cover and cook.
(vii) Mix the ground ginger and chillies with little water and add.
(viii) When almost cooked add tomato, salt and sugar. Cover and cook. Don't cook it till too soft.

Navrattan Korma

Preparation Time : 30 minutes **Cooking Time : 20 minutes** **Serves : 6 to 8**

Ingredients

French Beans : 100 gms
Kesari Carrots (English) : 125 gms
Shelled Peas : 100 gms
Cauliflower Florettes : 50 gms
Paneer (cottage cheese) : 100 gms
Pineapple Slices : 4 (tinned)

For the Korma

Onions : 500 gms
Tomato : 250 gms
Ginger : 2 inches
Garlic Cloves : 16
Green Chillies : 8
Turmeric Powder : ½ tsp.
Red Chilli Powder : 1 ½ tsp.
Cashewnuts : 50 gms
Curds : 3 tbsp.
Malai or cream : 3 tbsp.
Sugar : 2 tsp.
Salt to Taste
Bay Leaves : 2
Green Cardamom : 4
Cinnamon pieces : 2
Oil : ½ cup
Lemon Juice : 1 tsp.

Method

(i) Cut beans and carrots to ¼ inch pieces.
(ii) Cut small florettes of the cauliflower.
(iii) Cut ¼ / ½ inch pieces of the paneer. Don't cut them too thick.
(iv) Cut pieces of the pineapple (squeeze juice out).
(v) Except pineapple boil all the vegetables separately with a pinch of soda.
(vi) Soak the paneer in hot water.

Korma

(i) Cut onion to pieces and boil them in water (strain after boiling). Later grind them to a paste in a mixer.
(ii) Prepare tomato puree (refer method no. : 3).
(iii) Grind the ginger, garlic and chillies seperately.
(iv) Grind cashewnuts to a paste, adding little water.
(v) The curds and cream should be beaten separately.
(vi) Heat oil in a vessel and garam masala (whole). Add ground onions and saute till golden brown.
(vii) Add 1 ½ cup water and cook.
(viii) Add the salt and sugar.
(ix) Add curds, then turmeric powder.
(x) Add ground ginger, garlic and chillies.
(xi) Add tomato puree and let it cook.
(xii) Add red chilli powder and ½ cup water. Let it cook.
(xiii) Add ground cashewnuts and 2 cups of water.
(xiv) Add vegetables, cottage cheese and pineapple pieces and mix well.
(xv) Add beaten malai or fresh cream.
(xvi) Add lemon juice.

***Important Note :** Before adding lemon juice, taste to see if the tomatoes are sour. Then add lemon juice accordingly.*

Khava Mattar (Green Peas)

Preparation Time : 15 minutes **Cooking Time : 15 minutes** **Serves : 6**

Ingredients

Shelled Peas : 250 gms
Khava : 200 gms
Tomatoes : 100 gms
Green Chillies : 3
Ginger : 1 inch
Coriander Powder : 1 tbsp.
Red Chilli Powder : 1 tsp.
Ghee (homemade) : 1 tbsp.
Salt to taste
Cumin, Asafoetida, Turmeric
For Fodni (tadka)
Chopped Coriander
Kashmiri Garam Masala : 1 tsp.
(Refer method no. : 1)

Method

(i) Boil the peas well, till soft.
(ii) Peel tomatoes and chop to small pieces.
(iii) Julienne the chillies.
(iv) Grind the ginger.
(v) Heat ghee in a vessel and add fodni ingredients. Add ginger, chillies and saute.
(vi) Crush the khava and add it. Saute till it becomes golden brownish.
(vii) Add red chilli powder and tomatoes.
(viii) After some time add the boiled peas. Add salt and coriander powder. Saute and add little water. Add garam masala. This vegetable should not be dry.
(ix) Sprinkle chopped coriander.

Important Note : *Place the tomatoes in hot water for some time. Then peel them.*

Bakar Bhaji (Red Pumpkin)

Preparation Time : 15 minutes **Cooking Time : 15 minutes** **Serves : 4**

Ingredients

Red Pumpkin : 500 gms
Green Chillies : 3
Red Chilli Powder : ½ tsp.
Tamarind : size of a beetlenut
Jaggery : 30 gms
Salt to taste
Charonji : 1 tbsp.
Oil : 2 tbsp.
Mustard, Asafoetida, Turmeric and Fenugreek Seeds for Fodni
Chopped Coriander

Masalas to be roasted (bakar)

White Sesame Seeds : 1 tbsp.
Poppy Seeds : 1 tbsp.
Dried Coconut Piece : 1 ½/ inch (grated)

Method

(i) Peel the red pumpkins and cut them to big pieces.
(ii) Chop the green chillies.
(iii) Chop coriander.
(iv) In little water soak the tamarind.
(v) Heat oil in a vessel. Prepare the fodni by adding mustard, asafoetida, turmeric and fenugreek seeds.
(vi) Add the chillies and pumpkin pieces and saute.
(vii) Cover the vessel and cook without water.
(viii) When half-cooked add salt, masala (bakar), jaggery and tamarind pulp and sprinkle chopped coriander on top.

Important Note : *This is a traditional Nagpuri dish. It is prepared with tender red pumpkin and cooked without peeling there skins.*

Raw Tomato Vegetable

Preparation Time : 10 minutes **Cooking Time : 20 minutes** **Serves : 4**

Ingredients

Raw Green Tomatoes : 300 gms
Onion : 1 (medium)
Green Chillies : 2
Coriander Powder : 1 tbsp.
Red Chilli Powder : ¼ tsp.
Salt and Sugar to taste
Coconut Milk : 1 cup (thick)
Mustard, Asafoetida, Turmeric for Fodni
Oil : 2 tbsp.
Chopped Coriander

Method

(i) Cut the tomatoes to big pieces.
(ii) Slice the onions.
(iii) Slice chillies vertically.
(iv) Heat oil in a vessel and prepare fodni with the mentioned ingredients.
(v) Add onions and chillies and saute (fry onions till translucent).
(vi) Add coriander powder, red chilli powder. Add chopped tomatoes, cover and cook till soft, on low flame.
(vii) Add coconut milk, salt and sugar.
(viii) Give 2 to 3 boils.
(ix) Sprinkle chopped coriander.

Soleev (Shelled) Moong

Preparation Time : 30 minutes **Cooking Time : 15 minutes** **Serves : 6 to 8**

Ingredients

Moong : 1 cup
Oil : 4 tbsp.
Mustard Seeds, Asafoetida and Turmeric Powder for Fodni (tadka)
Salt to taste
Tamarind : size of beetlenut

Masala to Grind

Fresh Grated Coconut : ½ cup
Red Chillies : 6 to 8 } to be roasted
Whole Coriander : 2 tbsp. } to be roasted

Method

(i) Soak the moong for 7 to 8 hours. Drain in a collander. When the water drains out transfer the moong to a cloth. Tie and keep aside for sprouting.
(ii) Add the sprouted moong (see that the sprouts are not too long) to lukewarm water. Remove the skin.
(iii) Heat oil in a vessel. Add fodni ingredients and let them splutter. Add the moong sprouts (skins removed).
(iv) Saute and add water. Cover and cook. The moong sprouts should remain whole.
(v) When the moong are almost cooked add ground masala and salt.
(vi) When it's cooked add tamarind pulp.
(vii) This dish should retain some gravy.

***Important Note :** To speed up of the removing the skins, lightly rub the sprouted moong in water itself.*

Palak (Spinach) Paneer

Preparation Time : 30 minutes **Cooking Time : 15 minutes** **Serves : 4**

Ingredients

Spinach : 3 bunches
Boiled Peas : 1 cup
Tomatoes : 2 (large)
Paneer (cottage cheese) : 250 gms (Refer method no. : 7)
Oil : 4 tbsp.
Melted Homemade Ghee : 4 tbsp.
Red Chilli Powder : 1 tsp.
Salt to taste

Masala to Grind

Onions : 2 (large)
Ginger : 1 inch
Garlic Cloves : 8
Green Chillies : 3
Coriander : 1 tbsp.

Method

(i) Remove the stalks of the spinach and wash well.
(ii) Cook it without water. Squeeze it lightly and then grind it to a pulp either on a grinding stone or in a mixer.
(iii) Cut the paneer to ¼ inch thickness and ½ inch square pieces. Then deep fry till golden brown.
(iv) Prepare tomato puree (refer method no. : 3).
(v) Heat oil in a vessel. Saute the masala till the oil begins to leave the sides of masala.
(vi) Add tomato puree and saute.
(vii) Add the ground palak, salt and peas and saute.
(viii) Add the fried paneer and let it cook.
(ix) Before serving on the table transfer to a bowl. Heat ghee, add red chilli powder to it and pour evenly over the dish.

***Important Note :** When fresh peas are not in season then you may avoid using them. Paneer available in the market can be used. If you do not wish to deep fry the paneer pieces, then after cutting them in the above mentioned proportions you can add them directly.*

Stuffed Brinjal (Type 1)

Preparation Time : 30 minutes **Cooking Time : 15 minutes** **Serves : 4 to 6**

Ingredients

Small Brinjal : 250 gms
Onion : 1 (large)
Kala Masala : 1 tsp.
(Refer method no. : 1)
Red Chilli Powder : ½ tsp.
Tamarind : size of a beetlenut
Jaggery : double the size of tamarind
Salt to your taste
Oil : 4 tbsp.

Masala to Grind

White Sesame Seeds : 1 tbsp. (roasted)
Poppy Seeds : 1 tbsp. (roasted)
Grated Dry Coconut : ½ cup (roasted)
Coriander : 1 tsp.
Cloves : 4
Cinnamon : 2 one inch pieces

For Garnish

Chopped Coriander

Method

(i) Slice the brinjal in the centre once, then once across it. See that the halves are intact. Then soak them in water.
(ii) Chop the onions fine.
(iii) Soak the tamarind in water and prepare a pulp.
(iv) Add ground masala, salt, kala masala, red chilli powder tamarind pulp, jaggery and mix well. Add a little water if required.
(v) Heat oil in a vessel and add onions and saute. Add the brinjal. Place a cover with little water on the vessel and cook the brinjal.
(vi) The above mentioned masala prepared with a little water should be added.
(vii) Prepare to serve on the table by garnishing with chopped coriander.
(viii) If you wish to stuff the masala then do so in the cut portions of the brinjals. After stuffing it add it to the onions.
(ix) While stuffing the masala should be thick.

Stuffed Brinjal (Type 2)

Preparation Time : 15 to 20 minutes Cooking Time : 15 minutes Serves : 8

Ingredients

Small Brinjal : 10 to 12
Fresh Grated Coconut : ½ cup
Chopped Coriander : ¼ cup
Onion : 1 (small)
Garlic : 6 (cloves)
Ginger : ½ inch
} ground
Red Chilli Powder : 1 tsp.
Kala Masala : 1 tsp.
(Refer method no. : 1)
Turmeric Powder : ¼ tsp.
Coriander Powder : ½ tsp.
Cumin Powder : ½ tsp.
Salt to taste
Tamarind : beetlenut size
Jaggery : double the size of the tamarind
Cashewnuts : 6
Sultanas : 25
Oil : 4 tbsp.

Method

(i) Wash the brinjal well. Cut the stalks into half. Hold the brinjal in your hand, the bottom part on top. Slice twice in a + sign on the fleshy part. Place this in salted water.

(ii) Heat one tbsp. oil in a vessel. Add chopped onion, grated coconut and turmeric powder and saute a little. Cover and cook for sometime.

(iii) Grind this mixture to a paste.

(iv) All the other mentioned masalas should be added to the above ground paste alongwith salt and mixed well.

(v) Soak tamarind in little water and prepare thick pulp. Let the jaggery dissolve in the tamarind pulp. Add this to the above mixture and mix well. Make small pieces of the sultanas and cashewnuts and add it to it. Mix well.

(vi) Stuff brinjals with this masala mixture.

(vii) Heat oil. In a (langdi) vessel add 3 tbsp. oil and place brinjals. Place a cover with a little water over it. In between sprinkle little water over the brinjals and keep turning them so that they cook evenly.

Important Note : *If you wish to cook the brinjals in a pressure cooker, then first saute them in a little oil, turn them 2 to 3 times. Then place them in the pressure cooker, when the whistle sounds, reduce heat and keep for 3 to 4 minutes, turn off the gas. You can also cook it in an oven or microwave.*

Patiyali Korma

Preparation Time : 20 minutes **Cooking Time : 20 minutes** **Serves : 4 to 6**

Ingredients

Cauliflower : 150 gms
Capsicum : 100 gms
Kesari English Carrots : 100 gms
Shelled Peas : 150 gms (1 cup)
Green Chillies : 1
Thick Garlic Cloves : 6 to 7
Ginger : ¼ inch
Onion : 1 (medium)
Turmeric Powder : ¼ tsp.
Garam Masala Powder : ¼ tsp.
Cinnamon Powder : ½ tsp.
Water : ¼ cup
Milk : 1 cup
Cornflour : 1 level tsp.
Salt to taste
Sugar : ½ tsp.
Chopped Coriander
Melted Homemade Ghee : 3 tbsp.

Method

(i) Cut medium florettes of the cauliflower. Peel the stalks.
(ii) Deseed the capsicum and cut them into medium size square pieces.
(iii) Make small pieces of the carrots.
(iv) Deseed the green chillies, chop them fine. Chop the onions fine.
(v) Grind the garlic and ginger separately.
(vi) Mix the ground garlic in the ½ cup water. Keep aside.
(vii) Parboil all the vegetables. Drain them in a collander.
(viii) Heat ghee in a vessel. Add onions and saute a little. (See that the onion does not change colour).
(ix) Add the garlic water and let the onion cook on a low flame. Add turmeric powder.
(x) When the onions are cooked and the smell of the garlic reduces considerably, add chillies and ginger and saute. Add all the vegetables. Add milk, garam masala, sugar, salt and cinnamon powder.
(xi) After some time, add cornflour paste prepared in water. Let it cook. Add salt.
(xii) While removing from the gas, it should retain gravy. Sprinkle chopped coriander.

Important Note : *This dish is not only delicious but also very easy to make.*

Kelphul Bhaji (Banana Flowers)

Preparation Time : 30 minutes **Cooking Time : 15 minutes** **Serves : 4 to 6**

Ingredients

Kelphul : 1 (medium)
Onions : 2 (medium)
Buttermilk : 1 cup
Water : 1 cup
Green Chillies : 3
White Peas : 2 tbsp. (optional)
Salt to taste
Little Jaggery
Oil : 3 tbsp.
Turmeric Powder : ¼ tsp.
Fresh Grated Coconut : ¼ cup
Chopped Coriander
Saraswat Masala : ½ tsp.
(Refer method no. : 1)

Method

(i) Clean the kelphul well and chop them fine.
(ii) Mix together buttermilk and water. Add chopped kelphul to it.
(iii) Soak the white peas overnight (optional).
(iv) Chop the onions fine.
(v) Slice the chillies vertically.
(vi) Wash the kelphul, 2 to 3 times with water.
(vii) Cook the white peas and kelphul seperately in the pressure cooker.
(viii) Heat oil in a vessel. Add onions, chillies and saute. Add turmeric add the cooked kelphul and the white peas (optional).
(ix) Add salt, jaggery, coconut and coriander and let it cook for sometime. Add the saraswat masala and stir.

Important Note : *If you wish to prepare this dish for lunch, then you should soak the chopped kelphul over night in water and buttermilk mixture.*

Vegetable Jaipuri

Preparation Time : 20 to 25 minutes Cooking Time : 20 minutes Serves : 4

Ingredients

Gravy

Onions : 250 gms
Bay Leaves : 2
Cloves : 2
Cinnamon Pieces (1") : 2
Cardamoms (big) : 2
Ground Garlic : 1 tsp.
Ground Ginger : ½ tsp.
Red Chilli Powder : ¾ tsp.
Whole Coriander Powder : 1 tsp.
Castor Sugar : 1 tsp.
Mace Powder : ¼ tsp. (level)
Cardamom Powder : ¼ tsp. (level)
8 to 10 Cashewnuts
Fresh Cream or Beaten Malai : ½ cup
Thick Beaten Curds : 1 cup
Garam Masala : ½ tsp. (Refer method no. : 1)
Salt to taste
4 to 6 tbsp. of oil

Vegetable

Cabbage : 100 gms
Carrot : 1 (medium size)
French Beans : 8 to 10
Sultanas : 1 tbsp.
Cashewnuts : 6
Tutti-Frooti : 1 tbsp.*
Small Dried Alubukhara : 4 to 5 *
Melted Ghee : 2 tsp.

* Available in the market

Gravy

(i) Soak cashewnuts in water and grind to a fine paste.
(ii) Cut onions to pieces. Add them to a vessel with eough water to submerge them and cook them till soft. Grnd in a mixer to a paste.
(iii) Heat oil in a vessel. Ad all ingredients from bay leaves to big cardamoms (garam-masala). When they splutter add ground onion paste andsaute till somewhat golden brown.
(iv) Add 1 table spoon water to ginger-garlic paste. Add to onion mixture and saute.
(v) Add coriander powder and saute. Add red chilli powder and saute a little.
(vi) Add salt. Add 1 cup water and bring to boil. Turn off gas. Add beaten curds and mix well. Switch on the gas and continue on a low flame till oil begins to leave on all sides. Saute and let it cook.
(vii) Add cashew paste, cream or malai, sugar. Mix this well and let it bubble.
(viii) Add mace powder, cardamom powder and garam masala.

Vegetable

(i) Shred cabbage, cut carrots into 1 ½" pieces horizontaly. Grate them vertically. Grate in one direction only. Shred french beans to 2" long thin shreds.
(ii) Make pieces of cashewnuts.
(iii) Soak tutti-frooti in water.
(iv) Saute cabbage in ghee. Add carrots and beans and saute, cover and cook till somewhat soft. If required sprinkle water.
(v) Add cashew pieces, sultanas, tutti-frooti and alubukhara. Add gravy and give 4-5 boils. If required add red chilli powder and salt.

Fancy Batatawada, Vermicilli Upma and Quick Idli Quick Chutney

Sol kadhi

Tavaa Paneer (Cottage Cheese)

Preparation Time : 15 minutes **Cooking Time : 20 minutes** **Serves : 2 to 3**

Ingredients

Gravy

Tomatoes : 250 gms
Ground Garlic : ½ tsp.
Ground Ginger : ½ tsp.
Green Chillies : 2
Red Chilli Powder : ½ tsp.
Cloves : 3
Green Cardamoms : 3
Salt as per taste
Amul Butter : 2 tbsp.
Fresh Cream : 2 tbsp.
Honey : 1 to 2 tsp.

Paneer

Paneer (cottage cheese) : 150 gms
Finely chopped Onion : 50 gms (¼ cup)
Carom or Ajwain or Thymol Seeds : ¼ tsp.
Finely chopped or grated Ginger : ½ tsp.
Green Chilli : 1
Red Chilli Powder : ¼ tsp.
Whole Coriander Powder :¼ tsp.
Garam Masala : ½ tsp. (Refer method no. : 1)
Chopped Coriander
Oil : 1 tbsp.

Method

Gravy

(i) Chop tomatoes and chillies fine.
(ii) Mix tomatoes, chillies, ground ginger-garlic, red chilli powder, salt, cloves and green cardamom together. Add 1 cup water and cook till soft. It should be thick like a sauce.
(iii) Grind the above mixture in a mixer and strain it.
(iv) Transfer the mixture into a vessel. Heat after adding butter and cream. Switch off the gas. Add honey, mix well. Switch off gas after adding cream and butter and don't cook as the ghee will begin to leave the mixture.

Paneer

(i) Make paneer pieces ¼" thick, ½" in length and ¼" in breadth.
(ii) Chop green chillies fine.
(iii) Heat oil in a vessel. Add carom seeds. When it begins to splutter add onion, ginger and chillies and saute.
(iv) Add coriander powder and red chilli powder and saute.
(v) Add paneer pieces and saute.
(vi) Add the ready gravy. Saute till it becomes thickish. If required add red chilli powder and salt. Switch off gas.
(vii) Add garam masala and sprinkle chopped coriander.

***Important Note :** Prepare gravy in advance. Keep the cottage cheese ingredients ready. Before serving on the table proceed from method no : 3 and then serve it. Do not heat it over and over as ghee will begin to leave the sides of gravy.*

Rajma (Kidney Beans) in Tomato Gravy

Preparation Time : 30 minutes **Cooking Time : 15 minutes** **Serves : 3 to 4**

Ingredients

Kidney Beans : ½ cup
Tomatoes : 2 to 3 (medium)
Ginger : ¾ inch
Whole Coriander Powder : 1 tsp.
Green Chillies : 2
Red Chilli Powder : ½ tsp.
Chopped Coriander
Salt to taste
Oil : 2 to 3 tbsp.
Cumin Seeds : ¼ tsp.

Method

(i) Soak kidney beans overnight in water.
(ii) Pressure cook the soaked beans for ½ an hour. Drain and keep the water aside.
(iii) Grind tomato alongwith skins in the mixer and strain.
(iv) Grate ginger and slice chillies.
(v) Heat oil in a vessel. Add cumin. Add chillies, ginger and coriander and saute.
(vi) Add tomato puree. Saute till oil begins to leave the sides.
(vii) Add whole coriander powder and red chilli powder and saute.
(viii) Add kidney beans and saute. Add salt.
(ix) Add the beans water kept aside earlier, little by little and continue to cook till you get enough gravy.

Quick Bhindi (Okra)

Preparation Time : 15 minutes **Cooking Time : 5 minutes** **Serves : 2**

Ingredients

Bhindi : 250 gms
(not rainy season variety)
Ground Ginger : little less than ½ tsp.
Ground Garlic : little less than ½ tsp.
Salt as per taste
Desiccated Coconut : ¼ cup*
Ground Green Chillies paste as per taste
Oil to fry

* Available in market

Method

(i) Wash bhindi and wipe them dry.
(ii) Make 1" pieces of bhindi.
(iii) Mix ginger, garlic and green chilli pastes together.
(iv) Deep fry bhindi in oil. Drain excess oil on tissue paper.
(v) Apply salt to bhindi.
(vi) Apply the mixed masala pastes to bhindi.
(vii) Mix all the bhindi pieces in desiccated coconut.

Important Note : *Deep fry the bhindi on low flame so that the bhindi cooks.*

Cauliflower Bahaar

Preparation Time : 20 to 25 minutes Cooking Time : 20 minutes Serves : 4

Ingredients

For Cauliflower

Cauliflower : 250 gms
(medium florettes)
Lemon Juice : 1 ½ tsp.
Turmeric : ¼ tsp.
Little Salt

To Marinate

Ground Garlic : 1 tsp.
Ground Ginger : 1 tsp.
Red Chilli Powder : ¼ tsp.
Little Salt
Brown Vinegar : 2 tbsp.
Gram Flour : 1 ½ tbsp.
Cumin Powder : ¼ tsp.
Oil to fry

For Gravy

Finely Chopped Onion: 2 tbsp. full
Tomato Puree : ¼ cup
(1 medium tomato)
Almonds : 6
Sweet Curds : ¼ cup full
Mawa or Dried Milk : 50 gms
Whole Coriander Powder: 1 tsp.
Anise Seeds Powder :1 tsp.
Red Chilli Powder : ½ tsp.
Turmeric Powder : ¼ tsp.
Salt as per taste
Garam Masala : ½ tsp.
Saffron Threads : 10
Hot Milk : 1 tbsp.
Oil : 1 tbsp.

Method

(i) Remove the skins of the stalks of the florettes and wash well.
(ii) Add salt, lemon juice and turmeric to 2 cups of water. Boil florettes and strain in collander.
(iii) Mix ginger, garlic, salt and chilli powder together. Add 2 table spoons water and mix well.
(iv) Apply this to boiled florettes. Add brown vinegar. Mix well and keep aside for 15 minutes.
(v) Remove all the excess juice from florettes and sprinkle mixture of gramflour and cumin powder.
(vi) Deep fry all florettes till golden brown in oil.

Gravy

(i) Soak almonds in water. Remove skins and make a paste.
(ii) Beat curds.
(iii) Knead the dried milk powder (mawa).
(iv) Mix mawa, curds, coriander powder, anise powder, red chilli powder, turmeric, salt, together.
(v) Heat oil in a vessel. Saute onions till golden brown. Add almond paste and tomato puree and saute on a medium flame till oil begins to leave the sides.
(vi) Add curds and saute till the mixture has sauce like consistency. If required add more salt & red chilli powder.
(vii) Add garam masala.
(viii) Add fried florettes and let it bubble.
(ix) Transfer to a serving bowl. Sprinkle saffron and milk mixture.

Corn Curry

Preparation Time : 25 minutes **Cooking Time : 15 to 20 minutes** **Serves : 4**

Ingredients

Corncobs : 2 (large)
Coconut : 1 (small)
Onions : 125 to 150 gms or 2 (medium)
Tomatoes : 100 gms (2 medium) or 2 tbsp. ready tomato pulp
Ground Garlic : ½ tsp.
Ground Ginger : ½ tsp.
Cumin Powder : ½ tsp.
Coriander Powder : 1 tsp.
Red Chilli Powder : ½ tsp.
Turmeric : ¼ tsp.
Garam Masala : ¼ tsp.
(Refer method no. : 1)
Salt as per taste
Gram Flour : 1 tbsp. (level)
Oil : 3 to 4 tbsp.
Decoration
Chopped Coriander

Method

(i) Make 1" breadthwise pieces of the corn. Pressure cook for 20 to 25 minutes. While cooking add salt to the water.
(ii) Slice cooked corn vertically to get 4 pieces.
(iii) Chop onions and grind to a fine paste in the mixer.
(iv) Puree tomatoes (refer method no. : 3).
(v) Grate coconut. Extract thick and thin milk from it. The thick and thin milk together should be 2 cups.
(vi) Dissolve gramflour in ½ cup water.
(vii) Heat oil in a pan. Saute onions till golden brown.
(viii) Add ginger/garlic pastes and saute.
(ix) Add cumin/coriander powder and saute.
(x) Add turmeric and saute.
(xi) Add red chilli powder and saute.
(xii) Add tomato puree and saute well. Add little water and let it cook.
(xiii) Add gram flour mixture and let it cook.
(xiv) Add corn pieces and saute well.
(xv) Add thin coconut milk and bring to boil.
(xvi) Add thick coconut milk and give 4-5 boils, Add salt.
(xvii) Add garam masala.
(xviii) Before serving on the table sprinkle chopped coriander.

Important Note : *You can use Godrej or Kissan Tomato Puree freely available in the market. The corn should be tender. Dip the corn pieces in the gravy and eat it. By doing so, the gravy coats the corn piece and this tastes delicious.*

Methi (Fenugreek) Malai Mattar

Preparation Time : 20 minutes **Cooking Time : 15 minutes** **Serves : 4**

Ingredients

Finely Chopped Fenugreek : 1 cup
Shelled Peas : 1 cup
Tomato : 1 (large)
Onion : 1 (large)
Ground Ginger : 1 tsp.
Ground Garlic : 1 tsp.
Cashewnuts : 20
Malai or Cream : ¼ cup alongwith little milk
Ground Green Chillies : 2
Salt as per taste
Garam Masala : ¼ tsp.
(Refer method no. : 1)
Homemade Ghee : 2 tbsp.
Honey : 1 tsp.

Method

(i) Boil the peas till soft and while boiling add a pinch of soda.
(ii) Prepare tomato puree (refer method no. : 3).
(iii) Grate onions.
(iv) Soak cashews for a little while in water and grind to a paste in the mixer.
(v) Beat cream alongwith little milk.
(vi) Heat ghee in a vessel. Saute onions till golden brown.
(vii) Add tomato puree and saute.
(viii) Add ground ginger/garlic/chilli paste and saute.
(ix) Add chopped fenugreek and cook with little water till the fenugreek turns blackish.
(x) Add peas and salt and saute.
(xi) When it begins to bubble add cashew paste and beaten cream. Add honey and let it cook for sometime.
(xii) Add garam masala.

***Important Note :** Do not use the variety of fenugreek that is grown in the sand or the one that has thick leaves, for this recipe. Use the variety that is less bitter. You must definetely try this recipe. It is very tasty.*

Ribgourd Potato Vegetable

Preparation Time : 10 minutes **Cooking Time : 10 minutes** **Serves : 2**

Ingredients

Ribgourd : 250 (tender)
Potatoes : 2 (medium)
Green Chillies : 2
Cumin : ½ tsp.
Lemon Juice : ½ tsp.
Salt/Sugar as per taste
Oil enough for Fodni and a Pinch of Turmeric

Method

(i) Peel ribgourd and make 1" to 1" horizontal pieces of it.
(ii) Peel potatoes and make somewhat big pieces and flatten and crush them a little bit.
(iii) Grind chillies and cumin.
(iv) Heat oil in a pan and add turmeric. Add ground mixture and saute. Immediately add potato and saute. Cover this and allow this to cook for sometime. Add ribgourd and cover again. Add salt. Cover and cook. Add sugar and lemon juice. This dish tastes very different.

***Important Note :** Check the ribgourd for bitterness.*

Uttar Pradesh Dal

Preparation Time : 15 minutes **Cooking Time : 15 minutes** **Serves : 4**

Ingredients

Gram Dal : ½ cup
White Gourd : 250 gms
Onion : 1 (medium)
Tomato : 1 (medium)
Ginger : ½ inch
Red Chilli Powder : ½ tsp.
Garam Masala : ¼ tsp.
Salt as per taste
Cumin : ¼ tsp.
Oil : 2 tbsp.

Method

(i) Wash the dal well.
(ii) Peel gourd and make medium pieces. Chop onions fine.
(iii) Chop tomatoes fine.
(iv) Grate ginger.
(v) Heat oil in a pressure pan. Add cumin and onions. Saute till onions are golden brown.
(vi) Add grated ginger and turmeric.
(vii) Add dal and gourd and saute. Add tomato.
(viii) Add water and pressure cook (10 minutes)
(ix) Once it cooks add salt, red chilli powder and garam masala.

Dilkhush Stew

Preparation Time : 20 minutes **Cooking Time : 10 minutes** **Serves : 4 to 6**

Ingredients

Cauliflower Florettes : 100 gms
Potatoes : 100 gms
Carrots (English) : 100 gms
Corn (Tinned) : 150 gms
French Beans : 100 gms
Onion : 1 (large)
Coconut : 1 (medium) or
Instant Coconut Milk Powder : 5 tbsp.
Cornflour : ½ tsp.
Salt to taste
Sugar or Honey : ½ tsp.
Green Chilli : 1
Ginger Paste : ½ tsp.
Jeera Powder : ½ tsp.
Dhania Powder : ½ tsp.
Cumin Seeds : 1 tsp.
Garam Masala Powder : ¼ tsp.
Chopped Coriander
Oil : 2 tbsp.
Whole Spices
Pepper Corns : 3-4
Bay Leaf : 1
Cinnamon : 1" by 1" stick

Method

(i) Cut onion into large pieces.
(ii) Cut all vegetables into medium size and boil separately to cook lightly.
(iii) Extract one cup thick coconut milk and one cup thin coconut milk or warm 2 cups of water and mix in the coconut milk powder and cornflour. Blend well to avoid lumps.
(iv) Heat 2 tbsps. oil and add 1 tsp. cumin seeds.
(v) When they splutter, add chopped chilli pieces and the whole spices. Saute a little.
(vi) Then add the chopped onion and saute well till cooked.
(vii) Add the ginger paste, boiled vegetables and saute well.
(viii) Pour the coconut milk and mix well.
(ix) Add the salt, jeera and dhania powder, garam masala powder, sugar or honey. Mix well. Allow it to simmer for 2 - 3 minutes.
(x) Garnish with chopped coriander. This stew goes well with jeera pulav and/or parathas.

Soups, Salads and Chutneys

The preparation of the 'Koshimbir' or Indian Salad in our daily meals has been a long tradition followed from ancient times. It is normally served on the left hand side of the plate. While preparing the same, certain ingredients like curds, ground peanut, and ground mustard are very commonly used. This is basically a 'dressing', as it is commonly called in foreign countries. But foreign dressings are very different. They can be prepared and kept in the fridge for 15 days. Dressings of this kind are mentioned ahead in this book.

While preparing salads certain things have to be mainly kept in mind.

(i) The vegetables should be fresh
(ii) The vegetables should remain crisp

Some Important Notes and Decoration Tips :

(i) If you want the vegetables to remain crisp and fresh then soak them in cold water after adding a little lemon juice to them. Place this in the fridge and while adding them to the dressing remove them from the water.

(ii) If fruits like banana, apple etc. are to be used, then after cutting them accordingly apply lemon juice to the pieces liberally. This reduces their tendency of turning black.

(iii) While decorating the salad keep in mind that the decoration should be such that it can be eaten. Some examples :

(a) Before spreading the salad on a bowl or plate, first place salad leaves.

(b) You can prepare flowers by giving many cuts to spring onions vertically and then soaking them in ice cold water for a very long time.

(c) You can also prepare flowers from radishes.

(d) Peel carrots with a peeler to get thin strips. Place them in ice cold water and use them as curls to decorate.

(e) Cut the tomato slice to 4 pieces keeping the centre intact then bring the opposite points together in the centre. Place a piece of the green leaf of spring onion in the centre to give the effect of a butterfly. These are a few of the other forms of decoration that give a special look to the cuisine.

Cream of Tomato Soup

Preparation Time : 15 minutes **Cooking Time : 20 minutes** **Serves : 4 to 6**

Ingredients

Tomatoes : 400 gms
Carrots : 100 gms or 2 medium
Onion : 1 (small)
Turnip (shalgam) : 1 (very small)
Water : 2 cups
Salt as per taste
Sugar : 1 tsp.
Pepper Powder : ¼ tsp.
White Sauce
Milk : 1 cup (hot)
Water : ¼ cup
Butter : 1 level tbsp.
Flour : 1 full tbsp.

For Garnish

Grated Cheese or
Fried Bread Pieces

Method

(i) Chop the tomatoes fine. Peel and grate the onion, turnip and carrots.
(ii) Mix all of the above together and pressure cook after adding 2 cups water.
(iii) Grind all the cooked vegetables in the mixer and strain this through a strainer.
(iv) Prepare white sauce (refer method no. : 5). Mix together the tomato mixture and the white sauce. Add salt, sugar and ground pepper and mix well.
(v) Serve this soup hot.
(vi) Pour the soup in a soup bowl. Sprinkle grated cheese or fried bread pieces.
(vii) See to it that the soup is neither too thick nor too thin. If required, add water.

Cream of Carrot Soup

Preparation Time : 15 minutes **Cooking Time : 15 minutes** **Serves : 4 to 5**

Ingredients

English Carrots : 250 gms
Water : 2 cups
Flour : 1 tbsp.
Butter : 1 tbsp.
Milk : 1 ½ cups
Bay Leaf : 1
Chopped Onion : 1 level tbsp.
Salt and pepper as per taste

For Garnish

Bread Pieces Fried
Boiled and Sliced Carrot

Method

(i) Peel carrots and slice them fine.
(ii) Boil the slices well in water.
(iii) Keep aside 10 slices for later use.
(iv) Mix together milk, butter, flour and carrot slices, water and grind in the mixer, till they blend well.
(v) Heat little butter in a pan and saute onions.
(vi) Add 1 bay leaf and the carrot mixture and boil for 10 minutes. Add ground pepper and salt.
(vii) See that the soup isn't too thick or too thin. If required add water.
(viii) Serve the soup in a soup bowl. Sprinkle with fried bread pieces and 2 slices of carrots.

Velvet Corn Soup

Preparation Time : 5 minutes **Cooking Time : 10 to 15 minutes** **Serves : 6**

Ingredients

Cream Style Corn : 1 tin
Water : 4 cups
White Pepper : ¼ tsp.
Soya Sauce : 1/8 tsp.
Ajinomoto : 1/8 tsp.
Salt as per taste
Cornflour : 3 tsp.
Water : 3 tsp.
Eggs : 2 (large)
Milk : 3 tbsp.

Method

(i) Open the corn tin with a can opener.
(ii) Boil water in a steel vessel.
(iii) When the water boils, add corn mixture and mix well.
(iv) Add salt, pepper, soya sauce and ajinomoto.
(v) Prepare cornflour paste in little water and add to the boiling water. Allow it to cook a little (it should become shiny).
(vi) In a deep bowl beat egg whites with a fork till frothy. Add milk and beat again.
(vii) Add the egg mixture to the boiling corn mixture and stir slowly once. Serve immediately in soup bowls.

***Important Note :** You can prepare the soup in advance. But add the egg white mixture only while heating the soup before serving. Don't beat the eggs in advance. While adding the egg mixture to the boiling soup, switch off the gas.*

Spinach Soup

Preparation Time : 15 minutes **Cooking Time : 15 minutes** **Serves : 4**

Ingredients

Spinach Bunch : 1 (large)
Salt as per taste
Pepper Powder : ¼ tsp.
White Sauce
Milk : 1 cup
Butter : 1 tbsp.
Flour : 1 tbsp. (level)
Chopped Onion : 1 tbsp. full

Decoration

Fried Bread Pieces
Little Milk

Method

(i) Remove stalks from the spinach, wash and keep aside.
(ii) Boil and cook the spinach without water and grind in the mixer.
(iii) Heat butter in a pan and saute onion. Do not let the colour of the onion change. Add flour.
(iv) Proceed to prepare white sauce (refer method no. : 5).
(v) Mix together the spinach mixture and the white sauce. If required add little water. Add salt and pepper.
(vi) Serve this soup hot. Pour the soup in a soup bowl. Sprinkle bread pieces and add a twist of milk.

Sunshine Carrots

Preparation Time : 10 minutes **Cooking Time : 10 minutes** **Serves : 4**

Ingredients

English (Kesari)
Carrots : 4 (medium)
Sugar or
Brown Sugar : 1 ½ tsp.
Cornflour : ½ tsp.
Orange Juice : 2 tbsp.
Butter : 1 tbsp.
Pinch of Dry Ginger
Salt to taste
Water : ½ cup

Method

(i) Peel the carrots and make ¼ inch thick oval slices. Parboil them in water.

(ii) Cook all the mentioned ingredients except the butter. When it becomes thickish, remove from gas and add butter. Pour this mixture over the carrots and place them in the fridge. Sprinkle chopped coriander and decorate with carrot curls.

Carrot Beans Salad

Preparation Time : 15 minutes **Cooking Time : 10 minutes** **Serves : 4 to 6**

Ingredients

French Beans : 1 inch pieces -1 cup
Carrot Slices : 1 cup
Rajma (red kidney beans) : ¼ cup
Small Onion : 1
Little Chopped Coriander
French Dressing : ¼ cup
(see at the beginning of this chapter)
Butter : 1 tsp.

Method

(i) Soak the rajma overnight.

(ii) Cook the rajma well in the pressure cooker for ½ an hour.

(iii) Heat butter and saute the cooked rajma in it.

(iv) Parboil the beans and carrots in water after adding pinch of soda and a little salt to it. Drain in a collander.

(v) Slice onions into fine thin slices and seperate them in rings.

(vi) Mix the onions, rajma and vegetables together. Pour the French dressing. Mix lightly and keep in the fridge (for 2 to 3 hrs).

(vii) When this cools remove from the fridge. Spread in 3 distinct rows in a shallow oval shaped glass dish. Place onion rings on top and sprinkle with chopped coriander.

Peas and Onion Salad

Preparation Time : 15 minutes **Cooking Time : 5 minutes** **Serves : 4 to 6**

Ingredients

Shelled Peas : 2 cups
Pearl Onions : 1 cup
Flour : 1 tbsp.
Butter : 1 tbsp.
Milk : 1 cup
Salt : ½ tsp.
White Pepper : ¼ tsp.
Grated Cheese : 2 tbsp.

Method

(i) Boil the peas and onions.
(ii) Prepare the white sauce with the flour, butter and milk. (Refer method no. : 5). Add salt and pepper and mix well.
(iii) Add the white sauce to the onions and peas. Add cheese.
(iv) Place the salad in a oval shaped salad bowl.

Fruit Chaat

Preparation Time : 10 minutes **Cooking Time : 5 minutes** **Serves : 4**

Ingredients

Apple : 1
Banana : 1
Cucumber : 1 (medium)
Seedless Grapes : 100 gms
Potato : 1 (medium) (optional)
Salt and Chaat Masala to your taste (Refer method no. : 1)
Lemon Juice : 1 tsp.
Guava : 1 (small) when in season

Method

(i) Cut apple into ½ inch pieces with or without skin. Apply lemon juice to the pieces.
(ii) Peel the bananas and cut them to ½ inch pieces. Apply lemon juice to them.
(iii) Peel the cucumber and make ½ inch pieces of them and cut the guava to pieces.
(iv) Clean and wash the grapes.
(v) Mix all the fruits and place them in the fridge.
(vi) Before serving add salt and chaat masala. Toss it well till the masala coats all the fruits.

Important Note : *If possible prepare the chaat masala at home or, it is also available in the market. You can have this dish as it is or as a salad. If you don't skin the apples then it adds a splash of colour to the dish.*

Onion Salad

Preparation Time : 5 minutes **Cooking Time : 5 minutes** **Serves : 2 to 4**

Ingredients

Onion : 1 (large)
Salt, Red Chilli Powder and Pepper to taste
Lemon Juice or White Vinegar to taste

Method

(i) Slice the onions thinly and separate them.
(ii) Just before serving add all the remaining masalas.

Important Note : *If you add the salt, chilli powder before then it will become watery. This salad compliments chicken and mutton dishes and is very delicious.*

Pudina (Mint) Chutney

Preparation Time : 10 minutes **Cooking Time : 10 minutes** **Serves : 6 to 8**

Ingredients

Mint : 1 big bunch
Coriander : 2 handfuls
Onion : 1 (large)
Green Chillies : 3 to 4
Salt and Lemon Juice to taste

Method

(i) Remove the mint leaves and wash them well.
(ii) Make medium thick slices of the onions.
(iii) Grind the mint, coriander, chillies and onions to a fine paste.
(iv) Add and mix salt and lemon juice.

Dry Coconut Chutney

Preparation Time : 10 minutes **Cooking Time : 10 minutes** **Makes 1 Cup**

Ingredients

Grated Coconut : ½ cup
Raw Green Mango : 25 gms (small)
Red Chilli Powder : 1 tsp.
Jaggery : size of a beetlenut
Salt to taste

Method

(i) Grate the dry coconut.
(ii) Peel the raw mangoes and cut to pieces.
(iii) Add all the other ingredients and grind to make a chutney. Add some water if required.

Pineapple Carrot Toss

Preparation Time : 10 minutes **Cooking Time : 5 minutes** **Serves : 4 to 6**

Ingredient

Pineapple Tin : 1 (big)
English (Kesari) Carrot: 1 (large)
Sultanas : 1 tbsp.
Mayonnaise : 1 tbsp.
Salt and Pepper to taste

Method

(i) Drain out the syrup from the pineapple pieces.
(ii) Reserve 1 tbsp. syrup.
(iii) Mix the mayonnaise and syrup.
(iv) Grate the carrots.
(v) Soak the sultanas in hot water. Let them swell.
(vi) With a fork mix carrot, pineapple, sultanas and mayonnaise. Add salt and pepper. Keep in the fridge.

Dahi Palak

Preparation Time : 10 minutes **Cooking Time : 5 minutes** **Serves : 4**

Ingredients

Palak : 1 bunch
Curds : 1 cup
Sour Cream : 2 tbsp.
Salt and Green Chillies to taste

Method

(i) Remove the stalks from the palak and wash them well. Chop them and cook in a pressure cooker or outside without water.
(ii) When it cooks remove excess water. Crush it or grind it to a paste.
(iii) Beat the curds and cream well. Add salt and ground chillies and the palak and mix well.

Lemosa (Lemon Pickle Bohri Style)

Preparation Time : 10 minutes **Cooking Time : 30 to 40 minutes** **4 Jam Bottles**

Ingredients

Lemons : 25
Jaggery ¾ kg
Dates : 350 gms
White Vinegar : ¼ lit.
(1 ¼ cup)
Red Chilli Powder and
Salt to taste

Method

(i) Cook the lemons in the pressure cooker with their skins. Drain the water.
(ii) When they cool down deseed them. Grind the lemons and ½ quantity vinegar in a mixer to a paste.
(iii) If you are using black dates, then deseed and make small pieces. If you are using red dates then deseed them and soak the pieces in water for sometime.
(iv) Place the jaggery alongwith the remaining vinegar in a pan on the gas and melt it. Add salt and red chilli powder.
(v) Add lemon pulp. Cook till thickish. Add dates.
(vi) When it cools transfer in a pickle jar or bottle.
(vii) It is ready to eat after 1 day.
(viii) This is absolutely delicious.

Important Note : *If you taste this while it is hot, it may taste bitter but when it matures well, it does not taste bitter at all. Infact the skin of the lemon emanates an aromatic smell.*

Orange Onion Salad

Preparation Time : 15 minutes **Cooking Time : 5 minutes** **Serves : 4**

Ingredients

Oranges : 4
White Onion : 1 (medium)
Coarse Peanut Powder : 2 tbsp.
Salt and Sugar to taste
Little Green Chilli Paste

Decoration

Spring Onions : 2
Salad Leaves
Glazed Cherries : 4

Method

(i) Peel the oranges and deseed them. Cut into pieces.
(ii) Slice the onions fine.
(iii) Mix the orange pieces, onions, peanut powder, salt, sugar and chilli, lightly (do this before serving).
(iv) Remove the stalks from the spring onions. Prepare flowers, from the onions (see note at the beginning of this section).
(v) Arrange salad leaves on a dish and place the orange salad. Place the onion flowers on top.
(vi) Chop the glazed cherries and sprinkle on top.

Shahi Raita

Preparation Time : 10 minutes **Cooking Time : 5 minutes** **Serves : 4**

Ingredients

Seedless Grapes : 100 gms
Curds : 2 cups
Rose Water : 2 drops (optional)
Honey : 2 tbsp.
Cumin Powder : ½ tsp.
Pepper : ¼ tsp.
Pinch of Green Cardamom Powder
Rock Salt to taste

Method

(i) Clean and wash the grapes.
(ii) Beat the curds well.
(iii) Roast the cumin lightly and powder it.
(iv) Add the grapes, honey, rock salt and green cardamom powder to curds and mix well.
(v) Sprinkle pepper and cumin powder on top.
(vi) If you wish, add the rose water.

Eggplant Salad in Coconut Milk

Preparation Time : 20 minutes **Time : 10 minutes** **Serves : 4**

Ingredients

Eggplant : 300 gms
Coconut : ½
Salt and Red Chilli Powder to taste
Tamarind : size of a beetlenut
Jaggery as per taste
Oil : 2 tbsp.
Mustard, Asafoetida and Turmeric for Fodni (tadka)
Chopped Coriander

Method

(i) Apply oil to eggplant and roast on open fire.
(ii) When cool apply water to your hands and remove the skin of the eggplant. Crush the pulp.
(iii) Soak the tamarind in water.
(iv) Extract thick milk of the coconut (about 1 cup).
(v) Add red chilli powder, salt and tamarind pulp and jaggery to the coconut milk. Mix well. Add the egg plant pulp and mix.
(vi) Heat oil. Add fodni ingredients and pour on top. Add chopped coriander.

Roasted Gram Chutney

Preparation Time : 10 minutes **Cooking Time : 10 minutes** **Serves : 4**

Ingredients

Split Grams : 1 cup
Grated Dry Coconut : ½ cup
White Sesame Seeds : ½ cup
Red Chilli Powder : as per taste
Black Pepper : 6
Coarse Salt : as per taste
Asafoetida : 2 tsp.
Little Tamarind
Jaggery to your taste

Method

(i) On a low flame roast the split grams well. Grind to a coarse powder.
(ii) Roast the dry coconut and sesame seeds separately.
(iii) Pound the sesame seeds (see to it that no lumps are formed).
(iv) Pound the tamarind, jaggery and salt.
(v) Fry the pepper corns in oil.
(vi) Crush the coconut with your hands.
(vii) Pound this mixture along with the pepper corns.

Karnataki Chutney

Preparation Time : 15 minutes **Cooking Time : 15 minutes** **Serves : 4**

Ingredients

Fresh Grated Coconut : ½ cup
Chopped Coriander : ¼ cup
Green Chillies : 3
Ginger : ½ inch
Small Onion : 1
Fenugreek Seeds : 12
Tamarind the size of a beetlenut or some Lemon Juice
Sugar to taste
Salt to taste
Split Black Beans : 1 tsp.
Oil : 2 tsp.

Method

(i) Chop the onion fine.
(ii) In a small vessel heat oil. Add little mustard and asafoetida and split black beans. Saute and add fenugreek seeds. Let them turn light brown. Add the remaining ingredients (except tamarind, salt, sugar). Saute and remove from gas. Add salt, sugar, tamarind or lemon juice.
(iii) Grind on a stone or grind in a mixer. See that it's not too thick.

***Important Note :** This tastes very good with Idlis*

Fried Snacks and Other In - Betweens

Fried snacks are a great favourite in India. The amount and the variety of savouries that are made only go to prove this point. Fried snacks should be served hot. The cooking oil should be heated at first, on a high flame. The item to be fried should be let into the hot oil and when it puffs up, the flame should be lowered. This allows uniform cooking, right up to the core of the item being fried. Use a minimum amount of baking soda. Do not crowd the pan. This prevents improper frying, uneven colour and difficulty in turning over the pieces.

Always use refined oil for frying.

Onion Karanji (Turnovers)

Preparation Time : 25 minutes **Cooking Time : 30 minutes** **15 to 16 Karanjis**

Ingredients

Flour (maida) : 1 cup
Semolina : 2 tbsp. (full)
Homemade Ghee (melted) : 2 to 3 tbsp.
Salt to taste
Oil to fry

For Filling

Onion : 250 gms
Chopped Coriander : 1 cup
Grated Fresh Coconut : 1 cup
Salt, Green Chilli Paste, Sugar and Lemon Juice to taste

Method

(i) Mix the flour, semolina and salt well. Add hot melted ghee and knead to form a hard but pliable dough.
(ii) Grate onions and squeeze out excess water.
(iii) Add grated coconut, coriander, green chilli paste, salt, sugar and lemon juice to the grated onions and mix lightly.
(iv) Grind the flour mixture in a mixer.
(v) Make a small ball and roll out a puri. Place a little filling on one half of the puri and bring up the other side and close the edges, applying little water and then deep fry in oil till golden brown.
(vi) You can serve these with tomato sauce.

***Important Note :** Serve these turnovers hot. Do not prepare the filling mixture in advance as it may get soggy.*

Quick Bonde

Preparation Time : 5 minutes **Cooking Time : 15 minutes**

Ingredients

Chana Dal (grams) : 2 cups
Split Black Beans : ¾ cup
Moong Dal : ½ cup
Cumin : 2 tsp.
Coriander Seeds : 2 tsp.

Method

(i) Lightly roast all the dals and grind them coarsely, adding cumin and coriander.
(ii) Store this in an air tight jar.
(iii) Take it in the desired quantity and add red chilli powder, salt and little turmeric. Add little oil and make pakora mixture with little water.
(iv) Deep fry till crisp and golden brown.

***Important Note :** Since you can prepare the bonda mixture and store it, you can deep fry them in no time.*

Ragda Pattice

Preparation Time : 30 minutes **Cooking Time : 30 minutes** **12 to 14 Patties**

Ingredients

Potatoes : 500 gms
Bread Slices : 3
Lemon Juice : 2 tsp.
Salt to taste
Oil for frying

Ragda

White Dried Peas : 250 gms
Onions : 200 gms
Tomatoes : 2 (medium)
Green Chillies : 2
Red Chilli Powder : 1 tsp.
Oil : 3 tbsp.
Salt to taste
Cloves, Cinnamon, Cardamons : 2 of each

Masala to Grind

Whole Coriander : 1 tsp.
Fennel Seeds : 1 tsp.
Black Pepper : 15
Cinnamon : 4 one inch pieces
Cardamoms : 3
Cloves : 6
Garlic Cloves : 6 (large)
Ginger : ½ inch
Green Chillies : 3
Handful of Chopped Coriander

Liquid Chutney

Tamarind : 1 lemon size ball
Jaggery : 1 ½ lemon size ball

Method (Pattice)

(i) Boil and peel potatoes and grate and mash till soft.
(ii) Soak bread slices in little water.
(iii) Squeeze out excess water from the bread slices. Mix the potato mixture, bread, lemon juice and salt together and blend well.
(iv) Prepare 12 to 14 equal parts of the above mixture. Make patties and deep fry in oil till golden brown. (Fry the patties when the ragda is ready and just before serving).

Ragda

(i) Soak the white dried peas overnight.
(ii) Cook them in the pressure cooker the following morning.
(iii) Remove water from the peas and keep aside.
(iv) Apply the ground masala to the peas well. Add a little turmeric.
(v) Grate onions. Blanch tomatoes. Remove skins and chop them fine.
(vi) Chop the green chillies fine.
(vii) Heat oil in a skillet. Add cinnamon, cloves and cardamom.
(viii) Add onion and green chillies and saute till golden brown.
(ix) Add tomato and saute. Add red chilli powder.
(x) Add the peas.
(xi) Add the water that was kept aside. Let the gravy be on the thinner side. If required add more water.
(xii) Add salt and mix well.

Liquid Chutney

(i) Prepare tamarind pulp after soaking tamarind in water
(ii) Add jaggery to the tamarind pulp alongwith little salt and mix well.
(iii) In a shallow serving dish place the pattice first. Pour ragda over it and little chutney over it. You can also sprinkle fine onion slices if you wish. Serve hot.

Important : *Instead of soaking the bread in water, your can dry grind the slices in a mixer.*

Cabbage Bhanole (Cakes)

Preparation Time : 20 minutes **Cooking Time : 30 minutes** **20 to 25 Cakes**

Ingredients

Cabbage : 250 gms
Split Grams : ½ cup
Gram Flour : ½ cup full
Coconut Milk : ½ cup
Grated Coconut : 2 tbsp.
Cashewnuts : 10
Shelled Peas : ½ cup
Turmeric Powder : ¼ tsp.
Cinnamon Powder : 1 tsp.
Pepper : ½ tsp.
Coriander Powder : 2 tsp.
Cumin Powder : 1 tsp.
Red Chilli Powder : 1 ½ tsp.
Soda Bicarb : ½ tsp.
Salt to taste
Oil : ½ cup

Method

(i) Soak the split grams for 3 to 4 hours. Grind them coarsely (semolina consistency).
(ii) Chop the cabbage fine or grate them.
(iii) Break cashews to small pieces.
(iv) Parboil the peas.
(v) Mix the cabbage, peas, all other ingredients (including oil) to form a dropping consistency. If required add little water.
(vi) Grease a 9"/11"/1" square cake tin with oil.
(vii) Pour in the cabbage mixture.
(viii) Bake at 150°C for 30 minutes.
(ix) Cut squares (1 ½" × 1 ½").

Peas Karanji

Preparation Time : 10 minutes **Cooking Time : 20 minutes** **15 to 16 Karanjis**

Ingredients

Flour : 1 cup
Semolina : 2 tbsp.
Melted Homemade Ghee : 3 tbsp.
Salt to taste
Oil to fry

Filling

Peas : 500 gms
Salt, Green Chilli Paste, Sugar, Lemon Juice to taste
Chopped Coriander, little grated Fresh Coconut
Oil : 2 tbsp.
Mustard and Asafoetida for Fodni (tadka)

Method

(i) Shell the peas.
(ii) Crush the peas coarsely by pounding.
(iii) Heat oil in a vessel. Add fodni ingredients and let them splutter. Add peas, saute and cover.
(iv) Add salt, green chilli paste, sugar, lemon juice and mix. After two to three minutes add grated coconut and coriander. Mix well and remove from gas to cool.
(v) Proceed further as for onion karanji. The filling should be of peas, instead of onions.

Punjabi Samosa

Preparation Time : 20 minutes **Cooking Time : 30 minutes** **25 Samosas**

Ingredients

Flour : 2 cups full
Oil : ½ cup
Salt : 1 tbsp. (level)
Lukewarm water for making dough

Filling

Potatoes : 4 (large)
Red Chilli Powder : 1 tbsp.
Coriander powder : 1 tbsp.
Dry Mango Powder : 2 tbsp. or Lemon
Salt to taste
Cumin : ½ tsp.
Pinch of Asafoetida
Chopped Green Chillies : 8
Chopped Coriander
Oil : 4 tbsp. (for fodni)
Oil to fry

Method

(i) Add salt to the flour and mix well.
(ii) Heat oil and add to the flour. Rub in well.
(iii) Prepare dough with lukewarm water.
(iv) Boil and peel potatoes. Cool and chop to small pieces.
(v) Heat oil. Add cumin, asafoetida, green chillies and other masalas. Add potatoes and saute. Add salt, stir well. Add chopped coriander and mix well.
(vi) Divide the dough into 12 equal parts.
(vii) Roll out each to an oval of 8" × 4". Cut horizontally in the centre. Apply little water to the cut edge. Make a triangle out of it. Put the filling, close by crimping the edges. (See page 110 for illustration.)
(viii) Proceed likewise with others. Fry samosas till golden brown.

Vegetable Bombs

Preparation Time : 30 minutes **Cooking Time : 20 minutes** **Serves : 8 to 10**

Ingredients

For Covering

Potatoes : 500 gms

Bread Slices : 3 to 4

Salt to taste

Bread Crumbs : ½ cup

Filling

French Beans : 100 gms

Carrots : 100 gms

Shelled Peas : 100 gms

Cauliflower Florettes : 100 gms

Green Chillies : 2 to 3

Onion : 1 (medium)

Chopped Coriander : ¼ cup

Dry Mango Powder : 1 tsp. full

Coriander Powder : 1 tsp.

Salt to taste

Amul Butter : 1 tbsp.

Oil to fry

2 tbsp. oil for Fodni (tadka)

Method

(i) Boil and peel potatoes. Mash them.

(ii) Soak the bread slices in water.

iii) Mix together the mashed potatoes, salt and bread (squeeze to remove excess water).

(iv) Chop onions and chillies fine.

(v) Chop carrots and beans fine.

(vi) Boil the peas.

(vii) Cut cauliflower to small florettes.

(viii) Heat oil. Add onion and chillies and saute.

(ix) Add all the chopped vegetables and cook. Add boiled peas. Add coriander, salt and other masala and mix well. Set aside to cool.

(x) Make 8 to 10 equal parts of the potato as well as the filling mixture.

(xi) Roll out a puri of potato mixture. Put the filling in the centre. Put a small cube of Amul Butter in the centre of the filling. Prepare large bomb shaped balls (orange size). Roll in bread crumbs and deep fry till golden brown. Fry others in the same fashion.

(xii) Serve hot with tomato sauce.

Important Note : *If the vegetables are not fresh then parboil them. Instead of soaking bread in water you can dry grind them coarsely in a mixer.*

Cheese Pakoras

Preparation Time : 10 minutes **Cooking Time : 15 minutes** **25 Pakoras**

Ingredients

Flour : 1 cup

Grated Cheese : ½ cup

Amul Butter : 2 tbsp. (level)

Soda Bicarb : ⅛ tsp.

Green Chilli Paste and

Salt to taste

Oil to fry

Method

(i) Sieve the flour well.

(ii) Mix flour, cheese, butter, salt and green chilli paste. Add little water to prepare pakora mixture and keep aside for 2 hrs.

(iii) Before deep frying add soda and beat well. Deep fry in oil till golden brown. Serve hot.

Vermicelli Upma

Preparation Time : 15 to 20 minutes Cooking Time : 15 minutes Serves : 4

Ingredients

Vermicelli : 200 gms
Cashewnuts Pieces : ¼ cup
Green Chillies : 5
Turmeric Powder : ½ tsp.
Salt to taste
Sugar : 1 tsp.
Lemon Juice : 2 tbsp.
Grated Coconut : ½ cup
Chopped Coriander : ¼ cup
Oil : 4 to 5 tbsp.
Water : 1 cup

Method

(i) Break vermicelli to approximately 1 inch pieces.
(ii) Cut green chillies to pieces.
(iii) Heat little oil in a vessel. Saute vermicelli till golden brown and drain on paper and keep aside.
(iv) Saute cashewnuts till golden brown in the same oil.
(v) Heat oil and add mustard, asafoetida and turmeric powder. Add green chillies and saute.
(vi) Add salt, vermicelli and cashewnuts and saute. Sprinkle little water and cover and cook. Continue in this way till all the water is used. Add sugar, coconut and coriander and mix well. Add lemon juice and mix lightly.
(vii) The cooked vermicelli should be separate from each other.

***Important Note :** Preferably use Elephant brand, but any other brand will also do.*

Vegetable Burgers

Preparation Time : 20 minutes Cooking Time : 30 minutes 12 Burgers

Ingredients

Round Buns : 12
Amul Butter : 100 gms
Onion Slices : 12 (thin)
Tomato Slices : 12 (thin)
Salad leaves
Tomato Sauce : 12 tbsp.
Little Red Chilli Powder
Vegetable Cutlets : 12
(Refer : vegetable cutlets)
Tooth picks : 12

Method

(i) Slice each bun in the centre horizontally to make two halves.
(ii) Apply butter to the innerside of both halves.
(iii) Toast them till golden brown in an oven or grill (butter side up).
(iv) There are 2 bun halves—one flat, other dome.
(v) Arrange a salad leaf on the toasted flat half of the bun. Place cutlet on it. Place onion slice, then tomato slice on it. Spoon and spread 1 tbsp. sauce over it. Sprinkle red chilli powder and place the dome half of the bun over it and heat in a grill again. Pierce a toothpick through the centre.
(vi) Serve on a plate with potato wafers.

Amiri Khaman

Preparation Time : 20 minutes Cooking Time : 5 minutes Serves : 6 to 8

Ingredients

Split Grams : 1 cup
Salt to taste
Soda Bicarb : ¼ tsp.
Lemon Juice : 3 tsp.
Salt to taste
Castor Sugar : 2 tsp.
Oil : 4 tbsp.
Asafoetida & Mustard for Fodni (tadka)
Cashewnuts : 50 gms

To Grind

Ginger : 1 inch
Green Chillies : 3
Garlic Cloves : 8

For Decoration

Fine Shev : ¼ kg
Fresh Grated Coconut
Chopped Coriander

Method

(i) Soak split grams in water for 6 hours.
(ii) Drain in a collander. Grind the grams.
(iii) Add salt and soda bicarb to the grams and beat well. Add little water to the grams (to form dropping consistency) and cover for 2 to 3 hours.
(iv) Grease two shallow cake tins (thali).
(v) Pour water inside a steamer and place on gas.
(vi) When the water boils, pour equal quantity gram mixture in each tin.
(vii) Place tin in the steamer and cook for 15 minutes.
(viii) When it cools, cut to big pieces and grate.
(ix) Add ground masala, lemon juice, salt and sugar to 2 to 3 tbsp. water and apply it lightly to the grated mixture.
(x) Heat oil in a small vessel and add mustard and turmeric. Pour over the above mixture and mix well.
(xi) Cut cashewnuts to small pieces. Add to above mixture and mix well.
(xii) Before serving sprinkle shev, coconut and coriander lavishly.

***Important Note :** You can prepare the khaman in advance and heat before serving.*

Arbi Tikki (Collocasia)

Preparation Time : 20 minutes Cooking Time : 20 minutes Serves : 6

Ingredients

Arbi (collocasia) : 8 (large)
Red Chilli Powder, Salt and Cumin Powder
Oil to fry

Method

(i) Add salt to water and cook arbi in it till soft.
(ii) When it cools, peel the arbi and cut to 1 ½ inch pieces.
(iii) Deep fry these pieces in oil till golden brown and keep on a paper.
(iv) Press the pieces in your palms.
(v) Deep fry again and place on tissue paper for oil to drain.
(vi) Sprinkle, red chilli powder, salt and cumin powder on each. (Sprinkle when the tikki is hot so that the masala will coat it well).

Utappa (Andhra)

Preparation Time : 20 minutes **Cooking Time : 20 minutes** **Serves : 10 to 12**

Ingredients

Rice : 1 cup
Split Black Beans : ½ cup
Moong Dal : ¼ cup
Semolina : ½ cup fine variety
Onion : 1 (medium)
Green Chillies : 3
Ginger : 1 inch
Chopped Coriander : ½ cup
Salt to taste
Oil

Method

(i) Soak rice, split black beans and moong dal separately in water for 5 to 6 hours.
(ii) Grind each of them to a paste separately. Add semolina and mix well and let it ferment for 12 hours. The consistency of the fermented mix should be between dropping & pouring consistency.
(iii) Add little salt and mix well.
(iv) Before making the utappas, taste it and add more salt if required.
(v) Chop the ginger and chillies fine. Chop onions fine.
(vi) Grease a gridle with little oil and make utappas with the help of ladle. Don't spread the mixture. Sprinkle little ginger, chillies, onion and coriander on top. Place a cover. Turn over and cook the other side.
(vii) See that the utappa mixture is not too thin.
(viii) Serve utappas with chutney.

Patties

Preparation Time : 15 minutes **Cooking Time : 15 to 20 minutes** **10 to 12 Patties**

Ingredients

Potatoes : 250 gms
Rice Flour : 1 tbsp.
Salt to taste
Filling
Fresh Grated Coconut : ½ cup
Kishmish (sultana) : 10 to 15
Cashewnuts : 10
Chopped Coriander : 1 tbsp.
Lemon Juice : 1 tsp.
Kala Masala : ½ tsp.
(Refer method no. : 1)
Salt, Sugar and Green Chilli Paste to taste
Oil to fry

Method

(i) Heat water in a vessel and add little salt. Add potatoes and cook till soft. Drain in a collander.
(ii) While the potatoes are still warm peel and grate them. Mash and make it soft. Add rice flour and knead again.
(iii) Add salt to the potato mixture just before frying and knead well.

Filling

(i) Roast the coconut a little so that the water content reduces.
(ii) Chop the cashew to small pieces.
(iii) Cut the sultanas to two pieces.
(iv) Mix all the filling ingredients and add salt and masalas and mix well.
(v) Divide the potato and the filling mixture equally.
(vi) Flatten out the potato dough and put filling to prepare a ball. Apply little rice flour if necessary.
(vii) Prepare all the balls in this manner and deep fry in oil till golden brown.

Kelphul Cutlets (Banana flowers)

Preparation Time : 25 minutes **Cooking Time : 15 minutes** **15 Cutlets**

Ingredients

Kelphul : 1 (medium)
Buttermilk : ½ cup
Enough Water to soak the Kelphul
Salt to taste
Onion : 1 (medium)
Besan (gram flour) : 2 to 3 tbsp.
Red Chilli Powder : ½ tsp.
Oil : 2 tbsp.
Mustard, Asafoetida,
Turmeric Powder for Fodni
Oil to fry

Masala to Grind

Poppy Seeds : 1 tsp.
Ginger : ½ inch
Cumin : ½ tsp.
Turmeric Powder : ¼ tsp.
Cardamom : 1 (large)
Grated Coconut : 1 tbsp.
Black Pepper : 8 to 10

Method

(i) Clean and pick the kelphul and chop fine.
(ii) Mix the water and buttermilk together. Soak the kelphul in it for ½ an hour.
(iii) Wash the kelphul well. Add water and cook till soft in a pressure cooker. Drain out the water.
(iv) Chop the onion fine.
(v) Heat oil in a vessel and add fodni ingredients. Add onions and saute till golden brown. Add ground masala and saute. Add kelphul, salt and red chilli powder and saute. Let the vegetable become dry.
(vi) When it cools add besan and mix well. Divide it equally and flatten in your palms to form pedas. Deep fry in oil till golden brown.

***Important Note :** The required time to clean the kelphul is not included in preparation time.*

Quick Idli Quick Chutney

Preparation Time : 15 minutes **Cooking Time : 10 minutes** **16 Idlis**

Ingredients

Semolina : 1 cup
Curds : 1 cup
Ginger Paste : 1 tsp.
Salt to taste
Fruitsalt : 1 tsp.

Chutney

Curds : 1 cup
Peanut Powder : 1 tbsp.
Pinch of Asafoetida Powder
Salt and Red Chilli Powder to taste

Method

(i) Roast the semolina lightly.
(ii) Beat the curds and keep aside.
(iii) When the semolina cools a little add curds, ginger paste and salt and let it remain for 10 minutes. Add little water to form dropping consistency.
(iv) Add water to a steamer and let it boil.
(v) When the water begins to boil, add fruitsalt to the semolina mixture and beat it. Pour into idli moulds and place the idli stand in the steamer. Cover and cook. The idlis are ready in 10 minutes.

Chutney

(i) Beat the curds and add all the other ingredients and mix well.

Raw Banana Slices Shallow Fried

Preparation Time : 15 minutes **Cooking Time : 15 minutes** **15 to 20 Slices**

Ingredients

Raw Bananas : 3 (teen dhari)
Salt to taste
Red Chilli Powder : ½ tsp.
Little Tamarind
Rice Flour (coarse) : 1 tbsp.
Oil

Method

(i) Peel bananas and cut widthwise to form two halves. Cut each half to 4 slices lengthwise.
(ii) Prepare thin tamarind puree.
(iii) Sprinkle little salt on the slices and apply tamarind paste to both sides of the slices.
(iv) Add salt and red chilli powder to the rice flour. Coat both sides of the slices well in the flour.
(v) Add a little oil in the gridle and shallow fry them in a pan or gridle. Cover it.
(vi) Remove the cover and turn the slices till they become soft and change colour. Serve it hot. It tastes delicious.

Chana Dal (Split Grams) Cutlets

Preparation Time : 15 minutes **Cooking Time : 30 minutes** **16 Cutlets**

Ingredients

Chana Dal : 1 cup
Green Chilli : 1
Red Chilli Powder : 1 tsp.
Whole Coriander Powder : 2 tsp.
Turmeric Powder : ¼ tsp.
Garam Masala : ½ tsp.
(Refer method no. : 1)
Chopped Coriander : ¼ cup
Salt as per taste
Flour : 2 tbsp.
Water, Breadcrumbs
Oil to fry

Method

(i) Soak the dal in water for 4 to 5 hours.
(ii) Drain in a collander.
(iii) When the water drains out completely, grind coarsely in a mixer.
(iv) Add salt, red chilli powder, coriander powder, turmeric, garam masala, finely chopped chilly pieces and chopped coriander to the ground dal and mix well.
(v) Divide this mixture to 16 equal parts and make round balls.
(vi) Prepare a thick paste by adding flour to water.
(vii) Dip each ball in the flour paste, roll in the bread crumbs and press a little.
(viii) Deep fry all the cutlets in oil till golden brown on medium flame. You can also shallow fry them in a pan like palak cutlets.

Dudhi Handvo (White Pumpkin)

Preparation Time : 15 minutes **Cooking Time : 45 minutes**

Ingredients

Rice : 1 ½ cups
Gram Dal : ½ cup
Toor Dal : ¼ cup
Wheat : ¼ cup
Curds : ¾ cup (not sour)
Hot Oil : 2 tbsp.
Cumin Powder : 1 tsp.
Whole Coriander Powder : 1 tsp.
Turmeric Powder : ¼ tsp.
Sugar : ¼ tsp.
Salt as per taste
Soda Bicarb : ½ tsp.
Dudhi (white pumpkin) : 200 gms

Masala to Grind

Green Chillies : 5 to 6
Ginger : 1 ½ inch
Garlic : 8 cloves

Fodni (tadka) ingredients

Oil : 3 tbsp.
Pinch of Mustard, Asafoetida and Turmeric
Sesame Seeds : 1 tsp.
Fenugreek Seeds : ¼ tsp.

For Decoration

Sesame Seeds : 2 tbsp.

Method

(i) Wash the rice, dals and wheat well. Dry and grind to a coarse powder.
(ii) To the above mixture add curds and little salt. In the summer season soak it in lukewarm water for 3 hours, and in winter season for 8 hours in advance.
(iii) Grate the white pumpkin.
(iv) Except soda, fodni ingredients and sesame seeds for decoration, mix remaining masala, salt and grated white pumpkin to the mixture to form a dropping consistency.
(v) Heat oil, add fodni ingredients and keep aside to cool.
(vi) Add soda to the dudhi mixture and beat well.
(vii) Grease a cake tin (not very deep) and pour the mixture in it. Spread evenly.
(viii) Pour the ready fodni over it.
(ix) Sprinkle white sesame seeds over it.
(x) Bake in the oven at 150°C for 30 minutes.
(xi) Cut to square pieces.

Moong Kabab

Preparation Time : 20 minutes **Cooking Time : 15 minutes** **15 to 20 Kababs**

Ingredients

Moong : 250 gms
Bread : 4 to 5 slices
Onion : 1 (medium)
Coriander Powder : 1 tbsp.
Gram Flour (besan) : 1 ½ tbsp.
Green Chillies : 5 to 6
Lemon : 1 (small)
Dry Mango Powder : 1 tbsp.
Garam Masala : ½ tsp.
(Refer method no. : 1)
Red Chilli Powder : ½ tsp.
Salt as per taste
Chopped Coriander : ½ cup
Bread Crumbs : 1 cup
Oil

Method

(i) Soak the moong overnight.
(ii) Cook the moong in the morning (see that no water remains in the moong).
(iii) Soak the bread in little water.
(iv) Squeeze out excess water from the bread.
(v) Chop the onions and chillies fine.
(vi) Crush the moong.
(vii) Add the bread, chillies, coriander, onion, salt, other masalas and lemon juice to the moong mixture.
(viii) Add besan and make lemon size balls. Roll them in bread crumbs and press a little.
(ix) Heat little oil in a pan and shallow fry till the kababs are golden brown on both sides.
(x) Flatten the kababs and fry little more.

***N.B. :** Instead of soaking bread in water, cut up slices and make a bread crumb consistency in a mixer*

Suran (Yam) Kabab

Preparation Time : 15 minutes **Cooking Time : 20 minutes** **Serves : 6**

Ingredients

Suran (yam) : 250 gms
Potato : 1 (medium)
Chana Dal (split grams) : 1 tbsp.
Cinnamon Powder : ½ tsp.
Cloves Powder : ½ tsp.
Lemon Juice : 1 tsp.
Salt as per taste
Bread : 4 slices
Oil to fry

Masala to Grind

Green Chillies : 3
Garlic Cloves : 8
Ginger : 1 inch

Method

(i) Cook the suran, chana dal and potato in the pressure cooker.
(ii) Drain out all the water and grind it.
(iii) Add all the remaining masalas and ground masala, salt, lemon juice and mix well.
(iv) Soak the bread slices. Squeeze out excess water and add to the above mixture and mix well.
(v) Divide the mixture into 15 to 16 equal parts.
(vi) Make balls. Press a little and deep fry in oil till golden brown.

***Important Note :** If for some reason the suran mixture retains water, then spread it on a muslin cloth to drain before adding bread and other masalas.*

Gujiya Wada

Preparation Time : 30 minutes **Cooking Time : 30 minutes** **20 Vadas**

Ingredients

Whole Black Beans with skins or Chilka Urad Dal : 250 gms
Gram Flour : 2 tbsp.
Salt as per taste
Sultanas or Kishmish : 50 gms
Cashewnuts : 50 gms
Ginger : 25 gms (2 inch piece)
Green Chillies : 25 gms (8 chillies)
Chopped Coriander
Oil to fry
Curds : 1 litre
Red Chilli Powder and Salt as per taste

Method

(i) Soak the whole black beans in water for a minimum of 5 hours.
(ii) After it has soaked well, wash it well and remove skins.
(iii) Drain the washed dal in a collander.
(iv) Grind the dal in a mixer. Add salt and gram flour.
(v) Chop the ginger and chillies fine.
(vi) Cut the cashewnuts to small pieces.
(vii) Chop the sultanas as well.
(viii) Mix the ginger, chillies, cashewnuts, sultanas and chopped coriander together.
(ix) Beat the curds. Add salt and red chilli powder and keep aside.
(x) Spread a wet cloth and prepare thick puris of the dal mixture with your hands.
(xi) On one half of the puri spoon the ginger-chilli etc. mixture and bring both the edges together (like a karanji) with the help of cloth. Deep fry in oil and drop in a vessel full of water. After some time, gently remove and press lightly to remove the excess water and add to the ready curd mixture.

Palak (Spinach) Cutlets

Preparation Time : 20 minutes **Cooking Time : 20 minutes** **Serves : 8 to 10**

Ingredients

Potatoes : 1 kg.
Spinach : 8 bunches
Ginger : 2 inches
Green Chillies : 6
Red Chilli Powder : 1 tbsp.
Coriander Powder : 2 tbsp.
Garam Masala : 1 tbsp. (Refer method no. : 1)
Cumin Seeds : 1 tsp.
Pinch of Asafoetida
Oil : 4 tbsp.
Lemon : 1
Salt as per taste
Breadcrumbs : 1 cup
Oil to shallow fry

Method

(i) Cut the spinach (palak) stalks and pressure cook without water. Later crush it with your hands till soft. Drain out excess water.
(ii) Boil and grate potatoes.
(iii) Mix the spinach and potato together.
(iv) Chop the chillies and ginger fine.
(v) Heat oil in a skillet. Add cumin, ginger, asafoetida and chillies and saute. Add remaining masalas.
(vi) Switch off the gas. Add salt and lemon juice to palak potato mixture and mix well. Divide the above mixture to 20 equal parts and make peda size balls. Roll in breadcrumbs and press a little.
(vii) Shallow fry till golden brown on both sides by adding oil little by little in a skillet.
(viii) Serve hot.

Aloo (Potato) Tikki

Preparation Time : 20 minutes **Cooking Time : 15 minutes** **15 to 20 Tikkis**

Ingredients

Potatoes : 500 gms
Bread Slices : 4 to 6
Green Chillies : 3
Pomegranate Seeds : 1 tbsp. or
Lemon Juice : 2 tbsp.
Handful of Chopped Coriander
Breadcrumbs : ½ cup
Oil to fry

Method

(i) Boil and grate potatoes.
(ii) Soak the bread slices in little water.
(iii) Chop the chillies fine.
(iv) Squeeze out excess water from the bread slices and add grated potatoes, chillies, coriander, pomegranate seeds or lemon juice and knead it well. Add salt and mix well.
(v) Make small lemon size balls of the above mixture and press a little.
(vi) Roll them in bread crumbs and deep fry in oil till golden brown.

Important Note : *You can roll the tikkis in bread crumbs and store in a container in the fridge for one day. Fry them when required and serve hot.*

Cabbage Paneer (Cottage Cheese) Cutlets

Preparation Time : 25 minutes **Cooking Time : 15 minutes** **8 Cutlets**

Ingredients

Cabbage : 100 gms
Potatoes : 250 gms
Milk : ½ litre
Ground Pepper : ¼ tsp.
Salt as per taste
Little Green Chilli Paste
Jeera Butter : 6
Flour : 1 tbsp. full
Lemon : ½
Oil to fry

Method

(i) Curdle milk by adding lemon juice and make paneer. Drain out all the water from the paneer. (Refer method no. : 7).
(ii) Grate cabbage coarsely.
(iii) Boil, peel and mash potatoes.
(iv) Prepare a paste by adding flour to little water (not too thick).
(v) Pound the jeera butter to form a coarse powder (semolina consistency).
(vi) Mix the cabbage, mashed potatoes and crushed paneer and add salt, green chilli paste, pepper and lemon juice.
(vii) Divide the mixture equally into 8 parts.
(viii) Prepare cutlets by dipping each one in the flour paste and rolling them in bread crumbs.
(ix) Deep fry in oil till golden brown.
(x) Serve hot with tomato sauce.

Potato Peas Patties

Preparation Time : 20 minutes **Cooking Time : 30 minutes** **10 Patties**

Ingredients

Potatoes : 250 gms
Bread : 2 slices
Salt as per taste
Shelled Peas : 1 cup
Grated Ginger : ½ inch
Green Chillies : 2 (ground)
Dry Mango Powder : 1 tsp. or
Lemon Juice : 2 tsp.
Chopped Coriander : ½ cup
Mint : 3 sprigs
Salt as per taste
Breadcrumbs
Oil

Method

(i) Boil water, add potatoes and little salt.
(ii) When the potatoes are cooked, peel and grate them.
(iii) Soak the bread slices in little water. After they soften squeeze out excess water. Add the bread to the potatoes. Add salt as per taste and mix well devide into 10 equal balls.
(iv) Boil the peas. Remove excess water and crush a little. Add ginger, green chillies, salt, dry mango powder or lemon juice, coriander and chopped mint and mix well.
(v) Flatten each ball and put the pea mixture and prepare round patties.
(vi) Roll each one in bread crumbs, press a little to shape like peda and roll in bread crumbs again.
(vii) Add oil in a flat, thick bottomed pan and shallow fry cutlets till golden brown on both sides. Keep adding oil as required.

Paneer Cutlets

Preparation Time : 15 minutes **Cooking Time : 30 minutes** **10 Cutlets**

Ingredients

Potatoes : 1 kg
Lemon Juice : 2 to 3 tsp.
Bread : 8 slices
Salt as per taste

Filling

Paneer (cottage cheese) of : 1 litre milk
Green Chillies : 2
Chopped Coriander : ¼ cup
Dry Mango Powder : ½ tsp.
Red Chilli Powder : ½ tsp.
Garam Masala : ½ tsp. (Refer method no. : 1)
Salt as per taste
Breadcrumbs : ½ cup
Oil

Method

(i) Boil the potatoes.
(ii) Peel and grate them. Mash till soft.
(iii) Soak bread slices in little water.
(iv) Add salt, lemon juice, and bread (remove excess water after it softens) to the potatoes and mix well.

Filling

(i) Curdle milk and prepare cottage cheese in the usual way and crush it.
(ii) Except oil, add remaining masala to the crushed paneer and mix lightly.
(iii) Divide the potato and the crushed paneer mixture into 10 equal parts.
(iv) Flatten out each potato mixture part to form a small puri and add the paneer filling. Close the edges and form a ball and roll in bread crumbs. Press the balls a little.
(v) Prepare all the cutlet in this manner.
(vi) Shallow fry the cutlets in a thick bottomed gridle with oil till the cutlets are golden brown on both sides.

Shikampuri Kabab

Preparation Time : 20 minutes **Cooking Time : 20 minutes** **12 Kababs**

Ingredients

Refer to Pg. 90 — Suran Kabab

Take and measure all ingredients as mentioned in the recipe

Black Cumin : ½ tsp.

Green Cardamoms : 2

Fresh Grated Coconut : ¼ cup

Almonds : 6

Filling

Cottage Cheese : 100 gms

Finely Chopped Onion : 2 level tbsp.

Green Chillies : 1

Little Chopped Coriander

Little Chopped Mint Leaves

Salt as per taste

Method

(i) Grind black cumin to a powder.

(ii) Soak almonds in water. Remove skins and grind coarsely like semolina.

(iii) Heat a pan and saute grated coconut a little till it dries out.

(iv) Add all mentioned ingredients to the suran kabab ingredients and proceed as mentioned in the suran kabab recipe.

Filling

(i) Make very small pieces of the cottage cheese or crush.

(ii) Chop green chillies fine.

(iii) Prepare a mixture by mixing cottage cheese, chillies, coriander, mint, onion, salt together.

(iv) Divide into 12 equal parts.

(v) Prepare kababs with the filling (stuffing) in the centre and deep fry in oil till golden brown.

Fancy Batata Wada

Preparation Time : 20 minutes **Cooking Time : 20 minutes** **6 to 8 Vadas**

Ingredients

Vadas

Potatoes : 250 gms
Green Chilli Paste, Ginger
Garlic Paste as per taste
Salt as per taste
Lemon Juice
Chopped Coriander
Pinch of Sugar
Oil : 1 tbsp.

Fodni ingredients

Gram Flour : 5 to 6 tbsp.
Pinch of Soda
Fresh Curds (not sour) : 1 cup
Ground Ginger : ½ tsp.
Salt/Sugar as per taste

Chutney

Chopped Coriander : ½ cup
Chopped Mint : ¼ cup
Green Chilli : 1
Ginger : ¼"
Peanut Powder (coarse): 1 tbsp.
Salt/Lemon Juice as per taste
Pinch of Sugar

Decoration

Fine shev : 100 gms
Onion : 1 (medium) finely chopped

Method

(i) Boil and peel potatoes and cut to small pieces.
(ii) Add ground masala, salt, sugar and lemon juice, coriander. While sauting these together break potato pieces a little.
(iii) Prepare fodni with oil and mix with above mixture.
(iv) Add little salt and soda to gram flour and make a thickish batter by adding water and beat it.
(v) Prepare vadas out of potato mixture. Dip in gram flour and deep fry.

Sweet Dahi (Curds)

(i) Beat curds well. Add ginger, salt and sugar and mix well and keep aside.

Chutney

(i) Grind all ingredients to a fine paste in a mixer.
(ii) Add little water to make it a little thinnish. Place a hot vada in a serving bowl. Pour little curd mixture Spread a little chutney. Sprinkle onion and shev. This is very tasty and very different too.

Methi Muthia (Fenugreek)

Preparation Time : 10 minutes **Cooking Time : 15 to 20 minutes** **Serves : 2 to 3**

Ingredients

Finely Chopped Fenugreek : 1 cup
Finely Chopped Coriander : ¼ cup
Cooked Rice : ½ cup
Wheat Flour : ½ cup
Gram Flour : ¼ cup
Oil : 1 to 2 tbsp.
Small piece of Jaggery
Salt as per taste
Red Chilli Powder to taste
Coriander Powder : ¼ tsp.
Cumin Powder : ¼ tsp.
Anise seeds or Saunf Powder : ¼ tsp.

Fodni ingredients

Oil, Mustard, Asafoetida, Turmeric
Little Chopped Coriander and
Grated Coconut

Method

(i) Crush methi and coriander and add red powder, salt and mix well.
(ii) Add oil.
(iii) Add cooked rice (softened).
(iv) Add remaining powders and flour and with the help of water knead a dough similar to roti dough.
(v) Roll out 1" thick rolls.
(vi) Cook in pressure cooker for 10 minutes or steam in the simple cooker for 20 minutes.
(vii) After they cool cut out ½" wide slices.
(viii) Make fodni by adding little more than usual oil and add the ready fenugreek slices. Cover and cook. Add coconut and coriander.

Important Note : *Do not use fenugreek with thick leaves or fenugreek cultivated in the sand. Use fenugreek with round leaves. The rice can be a day old.*

Desserts

After a deliciously sumptuous meal, one always looks forward to having something sweet. Whether it is just an excess or a real necessity, one cannot really tell. But technically at the end of a meal, whether at home or at the end of a party, a dessert which is attractive to look at, mildly sweet and easy to digest is very welcome.

While deciding on a dessert a few factors have to be considered :

(a) the dishes served before, (b) the climate. During summer it would be wise to serve a dessert that is chilled and during winter something really hot would go well. In the same way if the dishes served during the course of dinner are very heavy to digest, then the dessert should be light, say with different types of fruits and ice creams or with other ingredients.

A few pointers to keep in kind while preparing desserts :

(i) For a party choose to prepare a dessert that can be made well in advance. If a dessert involves lots of intricate decoration or lots of time to prepare, then it would be a good idea to keep the dishes served during the meal, relatively simple. This would help you to spend more time with your guests. This is a better situation than spending most of your time in the kitchen.

(ii) Avoid using eggs kept in the fridge for puddings. They should be kept out of the fridge for an hour (at least) before use.

(iii) Always prepare custard on a low flame or prepare by Double Boiler Method (refer method no. : 2)

(iv) While beating egg whites, take care that no part of the yolk or even a drop of water enters it.

(v) While adding and mixing any ingredient to beaten egg whites do so with a light hand and mix in one direction only. This allows air to enter the mixture making it light and fluffy.

(vi) Keep the use of essence down to the minimum.

(vii) Use chilled fresh cream. Don't overbeat cream as it may turn to butter.

Chocolate Souffle

Preparation Time : 20 minutes **Cooking Time : 30 minutes** **Serves : 8**

Ingredients

Egg : 3
Castor Sugar : ¾ cup
Milk : ½ cup
Gelatine : 14 gms or 1 ¼ packet or 1 tbsp.
Water : 3 tbsp.
Plain Chocolate : 60 gms
Fresh Cream : 200 gms or 1 cup

Utensils

Souffle Dish (big enough to hold 3 cups of water)
One Tracing Paper

Method

(i) Prepare the souffle dish.*
(ii) Beat egg yolks and sugar together. In a vessel mix the milk and egg mixture together and by the double boiler method (refer method no. : 2) beat with a wooden spoon till light. Remove from gas.
(iii) Dissolve the gelatine in hot water and add to the above mixture and mix well.
(iv) Melt the chocolate on a low flame and add to the above mixture and mix well.
(v) Set aside to cool.
(vi) Beat the egg whites till thick and fluffy.
(vii) Add ¼ cup cream to the cooled chocolate mixture.
(viii) Add the beaten egg whites and mix lightly.
(ix) Pour this ready mixture in the prepared souffle dish and leave it to set in the fridge.
(x) When the souffle sets, remove the paper.
(xi) Beat ¼ cup cream till thick. Put into an icing bag and decorate the top of the souffle (optional).

** Method to prepare souffle dish : Take a tracing paper that is 4 inches longer than the diameter of the souffle dish and two times the height of the souffle dish plus 6 inches in length and width. Fold the paper lengthwise. Tie this folded tracing paper with a thread along the outerside of the souffle dish. If you want to present the souffle in this manner use a souffle dish as mentioned in the recipe. Otherwise you can use any bowl, big enough to hold the souffle mixture.*

Chocolate Sauce

Preparation Time : 5 minutes **Cooking Time : 10 minutes** **1 Cup**

Ingredients

Cornflour : 1 tbsp.
Cocoa Powder: 2 tbsp.
Sugar : 3 tbsp.
Water : 1 cup
Vanilla Essence : 3 drops
Melted Butter : 1 tbsp. level

Method

(i) Mix the cornflour, cocoa and sugar together and add little water and mix well.
(ii) Boil the remaining water. Add the boiling water to the cocoa mixture and mix well. Place this on the gas and cook for 2 minutes.
(iii) While cooking, stir continuously. Add vanilla essence and butter and mix well. Use as and when you require.

Lemon Souffle

Preparation Time : 20 minutes **Cooking Time : 25 minutes** **Serves : 8**

Ingredients

Eggs : 3
Castor Sugar : ¾ cup
Juice of 2 Lemons
Gelatine : 14 gms
(1 ¼ packet) or 1 tbsp.
Water : 3 tbsp.
Lemon Rind : 1
Fresh Cream : 200 gms

Utensil

Souffle dish big enough to hold 3 to 3 ½ cups water

Decoration

Walnuts and Glazed Cherries

Method

(i) Start by preparing soufile dish in the same manner as mentioned in the chocolate souffle recipe.
(ii) Dissolve gelatine in hot water.
(iii) Beat egg yolks, sugar and lemon juice by the double boiler method (refer method no. : 2) till light and fluffy.
(iv) Add lemon rind and gelatine and mix well.
(v) Proceed further in the same way as mentioned for chocolate souffle. Decorate with walnuts and chopped cherries.

Important Note : *If you don't want to prepare the souffle dish by using tracing paper, then use a souffle dish big enough to hold the mixture. You can decorate from the top. Both the dishes taste alike. Only, the souffle done with tracing paper looks more attractive.*

Mango Cream

Preparation Time : 15 minutes **Cooking Time : 15 minutes** **Serves : 8**

Ingredients

Tinned or Fresh Mango Pulp : 1 cup
Milk : 1 cup
Fresh Cream or Malai
removed from top of milk : 1 cup
Gelatin : 1 packet or 11 gms
Sugar : 5 tbsp.
Ice Cubes : 10 to 15
Utensils
Glass bowl : 1 or a souffle dish

Method

(i) Beat the fresh cream or the malai with a hand mixer till thick.
(ii) Mix the milk, sugar and gelatine together. Place on gas and melt them stirring continuously. Set aside to cool (under the fan).
(iii) Keep the ice cubes in a wide bowl. Place the bowl containing the cooled gelatine mixture over it and beat with a hand mixer till light.
(iv) Remove from ice and add beaten mango juice and beat again.
(v) Add cream and beat well.
(vi) Pour this mixture into a bowl or souffle dish and leave to set in the fridge.
(vii) It requires about 1 hour to set.

Important Note : *If your are using fresh cream then remove from fridge. When it softens beat till thick. But if you want to use homemade malai, then proceed as written below.*
Heat fresh milk on gas and when done, cover and keep aside and when it becomes lukewarm, keep in the fridge. After 6 to 7 hours remove from fridge and remove the malai from the top and keep in another bowl and keep in the fridge again. Remove after 1 hour and beat with a hand mixer. Keep in mind that while beating, don't beat too much otherwise it will form butter. You can use the cream to decorate, but it should be thick in consistency.

Orange Biscuit Flan

Preparation Time : 15 minutes **Cooking Time : 35 minutes** **Serves : 4**

Ingredients

Digestive Biscuits : 10
Amul Butter : 2 tbsp.
Condensed Milk : ½ Tin
Gelatine : 1 packet (10 gms)
Water : 2 tbsp.
Orange Juice : ¾ cup
Orange Colour : 4 drops
Orange Jam

Method

(i) Crush the biscuits evenly to form a coarse powder.
(ii) Melt butter and add to it.
(iii) Press the above mixture to the bottom of a cake tin and keep in the fridge.
(iv) Melt gelatine in hot water and set aside in a warm place
(v) Beat orange juice, condensed milk and gelatine together. Add orange colour.
(vi) Pour this mixture in the ready cake tin and let it set in the fridge.
(vii) Once the flan sets, beat jam and decorate the top.

Important Note : *To get the biscuit crush evenly, place biscuit pieces on 1 half of brown paper, fold the other half over it and roll with the help of a rolling pin to crush evenly.*

Strawberry Floating Islands

Preparation Time : 10 minutes **Cooking Time : 30 minutes** **Serves : 4**

Ingredients

Egg Whites : 2
Pinch of Salt
Castor Sugar : ¼ cup
Milk : 2 ½ cup
Egg : 3
Egg Yolks : 2
Castor Sugar : ¼ cup
Pinch of Salt
Vanilla Essence : 1 ¼ tsp.
16 Strawberries or 16 preserved Cherries

Method

(i) Beat the egg whites well till stiff and add salt. Beat it till stiff by adding sugar slowly enough (beat till stiff to form peaks).

(ii) Heat milk in a wide vessel. When it boils, with the help of a table spoon, take the egg mixture and spoon 8 long round balls into the milk. Reduce gas and let it cook for 5 minutes. In this way the egg balls will get stiff. Remove these cooked balls with the help of a perforated spoon and keep on a plate.

(iii) Beat 3 eggs plus 2 yolks, a little. Add sugar and beat again. Add this egg mixture to the above milk mixture and using a wooden spoon beat by the Double Boiler Method (refer method no. : 2) and prepare the custard. Remove from gas and add essence and mix well. When it cools down, transfer this custard to a wide transparent glass bowl and slowly add the set aside egg balls (islands) into it. Place a strawberry on each island. Make small pieces of the remaining strawberries and sprinkle them in the custard around the islands. Keep this in the fridge to cool.

(iv) While serving you can either spoon a little custard first into a glass serving bowl and then the islands or you can ask the people to serve themselves.

Important Note : *This dish should be adequately chilled. If you want to make this dessert when the strawberry season is over, you can use tinned cherries for decoration instead. These cherries are available in all routine stores.*

Melba Sauce (Raspberry Sauce)

Preparation Time : 5 minutes **Cooking Time : 10 minutes** **Makes 1 Cup**

Ingredients

Araroots : 15 gms
Water : 1 cup
Lemon Juice : ½ tbsp.
Raspberry Jam : 1 tbsp. full

Method

(i) Add the araroot in little water and mix well.

(ii) Add beaten jam and lemon juice to the remaining water and place on the gas to cook.

(iii) Strain the hot jam mixture into the araroot mixture. Mix well and place on gas. Remove from gas after 3 to 4 minutes and set aside to cool. Use as and when required.

Important Note : *You can pour this on ice cream scoops.*

Caramel Custard

Preparation Time : 10 minutes **Cooking Time : 10 minutes** **Serves : 6 to 8**

Ingredients

Caramel Sugar : 3 tbsp. full or
Sugar Cubes : 15 to 16
Water : 2 tbsp.
Lemon Juice : ¼ tsp.

Custard

Milk : 2 cups (½ litre)
Eggs : 3
Castor Sugar : 6 tbsp.
Nutmeg Powder : ¼ tsp.

Utensils

A jelly mould big enough to hold 2 ½ to 3 cups of water glace or Brown Paper and string to secure

Method

Caramel

(i) Prepare caramel in a thick bottomed vessel (refer method no. : 4).
(ii) Pour immediately in the jelly mould and rotate the mould with your hand to coat the caramel on all sides and the central depression evenly.

Custard

(i) Heat the milk.
(ii) Beat eggs and sugar in a vessel till light.
(iii) With one hand, slowly pour the milk into the egg mixture and with your other hand keep beating it with a wooden spoon. When half of the milk is poured, you can pour the remaining at once, but continue stirring. Add nutmeg and mix well.
(iv) Pour this into the ready jelly mould and cover with a paper and secure with a string.
(v) Place the mould in a pressure cooker. After one whistle, reduce the heat. After 5 to 7 minutes, shut gas. When the pressure falls, take it out and remove paper. When it cools invert in a dish with depth and let it cool in the fridge.

Ginger Pineapple Cream

Preparation Time : 15 minutes **Cooking Time : 20 minutes** **Serves : 4**

Ingredients

Pineapple Slices : 1 small tin
Fresh Cream : 100 gms
Ginger Biscuits : 8
Little Castor Sugar (optional)

For Decoration

Cherries & Pineapple Slices

Utensil

Transparent glass bowl

Method

(i) Drain out the syrup from the pineapple and keep aside.
(ii) Beat the cream till thick and add sugar.
(iii) Add the pineapple pieces to half portion of cream. Leave some pineapple pieces aside for decoration.
(iv) Dip each biscuit in the syrup and keep aside.
(v) Arrange 6 biscuits on the bottom of the bowl and pour the pineapple-cream mixture over it.
(vi) Make pieces of the other 2 biscuits and spread over it.
(vii) Pour the remaining cream and spread it evenly.
(viii) Decorate with cherries and pineapple pieces and place in the fridge to cool.

Apple Crumple

Preparation Time : 20 minutes **Cooking Time : 15 to 20 minutes** **Serves : 4 to 6**

Ingredients

Apples : 3 (large)
Brown Sugar : 2 tbsp. (level)
Cinnamon Powder : ½ tsp.
Lemon Juice : 2 tsp.
Lemon Rind : 1 tsp.
Water : 3 tbsp.

Short Crust Pastry

Flour : ½ cup
Butter : ¼ cup (frozen)
Castor Sugar : 2 tsp.

Method

(i) Peel and core the apples. Cut to small pieces and apply lemon juice.
(ii) In a vessel add apple pieces, brown sugar and water and place on the gas.
(iii) Cover and let the pieces soften. Add lemon rind and cinnamon powder and mix well.

Crumbs

(i) Sieve the flour.
(ii) Make small pieces of the butter and add to the flour. With the tips of your fingers mix the flour and butter to form semolina like consistency. Add sugar and mix well.
(iii) Pour the apple mixture in a pie dish and spread evenly. Sprinkle the flour butter mixture over it and press a little to level it. Bake in the oven at 150°C for 15 to 20 minutes or till it turns golden brown on top.
(iv) Make 6 equal parts of it.
(v) Place each portion in a glass bowl and add 1 cup vanilla ice cream over it.
(vi) While serving the apple crumple must be hot. Top with ice cream.

***Important Note :** If you don't want to cook the apple with brown sugar then use them as they are.*

Dates and Vermicelli Kheer

Preparation Time : 10 minutes **Cooking Time : 10 minutes** **Serves : 6**

Ingredients

Fine Vermicelli : 50 gms
Dates : 10
Milk : 3 cups
Sugar : 8 tsp.
Cinnamon : 2 pieces
Homemade Ghee :1 tbsp.
Cinnamon Powder: ½ tsp.

Method

(i) Make 2 to 3 inch pieces of the vermicelli.
(ii) Deseed the dates and cut them to pieces.
(iii) In a vessel, heat ghee and add cinnamon pieces.
(iv) Add the vermicelli and saute.
(v) Add little water and give 2 boils. Add milk and sugar. Add dates and cinnamon powder.
(vi) Don't let the vermicelli become too soft, the vermicelli pieces should be separate from each other.
(vii) Serve this kheer chilled or lukewarm.

***Important Note :** If you wish to serve this as a dessert, then cook till the kheer is thickish and chill. If you want to serve it with rotis, then it shouldn't be too thick. So vary the quantity of milk accordingly.*

Pineapple Pudding

Preparation Time : 20 minutes **Cooking Time : 20 minutes** **Serves : 8 to 10**

Ingredients

Pineapple : 1 (large)
Sugar : 250 gms
Cornflour : 3 tbsp.
Milk : ½ cup
Cream : 300 gms
Seedless Strawberry Jam : ¼ cup
Pineapple Essence : few drops

Method

(i) Slice the pineapple vertically into 2 halves along with the leaves.
(ii) Remove all the pulp from the halves and keep aside. Keep the empty shells along with the leaves and keep in the fridge to cool.
(iii) Cut the pineapple pulp to small pieces. Add sugar and cook it in a vessel.
(iv) Prepare cornflour paste in milk and add to the pineapple mixture. Cook for sometime. Remove from gas and set aside to cool.
(v) Beat till thick. Add essence.
(vi) Add 200 grams cream to the pineapple mixture and mix well.
(vii) Pour the above mixture into both the pineapple shells.
(viii) Spread the remaining cream over the top evenly.
(ix) Beat the jam.Transfer into a paper icing bag and decorate the top of the pudding. Keep in the fridge to chill.

Important Note : *For this recipe use a pineapple which is over 1 ½ kg or the pulp removed should be 2 ½ to 3 cups. If the pineapple is smaller then vary the quantity of the ingredients accordingly.*

Nutty Chocolate Sundae

Preparation Time : 15 minutes **Cooking Time : 10 minutes** **Serves : 6**

Ingredients

Vanilla Ice Cream Cups : 6 (large)
Cashewnuts : 50 grams
Dry Grated Coconut : 6 tbsp.
Milk Chocolate : 1 big slab
Amul Butter : 1 tsp.

Method

(i) Set the fridge temperature to coldest.
(ii) Keep the ice cream cups in the freezer.
(iii) Roast the dry coconut till golden brown.
(iv) Deep fry the cashewnuts till golden brown, in oil or ghee. Crush to form thick pieces.
(v) Place the chocolate slabs in a vessel on the gas and melt the chocolate. Keep stirring continuously.
(vi) When it melts add butter. Remove from gas.
(vii) The serving glass should be transparent.
(viii) This dessert is usually served in an ice cream bowl or in a tall glass.
(ix) While serving, scoop one ice cream cup in the glass. Then pour chocolate sauce over it and sprinkle cashewnuts and coconut.

Important Note : *If you keep the ingredients ready in advance, then it hardly takes any time and it is also very delicious.*

Orange Delight

Preparation Time : 20 minutes **Cooking Time : 30 minutes** **Serves : 6 to 8**

Ingredients

Orange Jelly : 1 packet
Oranges : 4 to 5 (large)
Milk Chocolate: 1 medium slab
Vanilla Ice Cream: 4 large cups
Sugar as per taste
Water : 2 cups
Little Orange Colour
½ Glaze Paper

Method

(i) Extract the juice of 3 oranges.
(ii) Peel the remaining oranges and cut the segments into pieces.
(iii) Mix 1 cup water and ½ cup orange juice together.
(iv) Heat 1 cup water and dissolve 1 packet orange jelly in it.
(v) Mix together the juice, jelly and the ice cream well.
(vi) Pour the above into a big wide glass bowl and keep in the fridge to set.
(vii) Cut glaze paper to form 1 inch strips.
(viii) When the mixture sets, place the strips at a distance of 1 inch from each other diagonally.
(ix) Grate the chocolate slab (from the fridge) and sprinkle in the space between the strips.
(x) Remove strips and place orange pieces in their place.

Trifle Pudding

Preparation Time : 15 minutes **Cooking Time : 20 minutes** **Serves : 10**

Ingredients

Sponge Cake : 300 gms (readymade)
Jam : 2 tbsp.
Fruit Juice : 1 cup
Wine or Rum : 2 tbsp. (optional)
Milk : 2 cups
Water : ½ cup
Sugar : 4 tsp.
Custard Powder : 2 tbsp.
Fruit Cocktail : 1 large tin or 2 Oranges, 2 Chickoos, 1 Banana, ½ cup Grapes, 1 to 2 Apples
Tinned Pineapple : 3 slices
Fresh Cream : 50 gms
Cherries : 6
Castor Sugar : 1 tsp.

Utensils

Souffle dish or glass bowl big enough to hold 6 cups water

Method

(i) Slice the cake horizontally to form 2 halves.
(ii) Beat jam and apply to both slices evenly.
(iii) Place both the slices (jam side inside) on top of each other in a cake bowl and cut to form pieces.
(iv) Add rum or wine to juice and pour over cake evenly.
(v) If you don't want to use rum or wine, just pour juice.
(vi) Prepare custard by mixing custard powder, sugar, milk and water and keep aside to cool.
(vii) Beat cream till somewhat thick and add sugar.
(viii) If you are using fresh fruits, peel them, cut to small pieces and add sugar.
(ix) If you are using tinned fruits, then drain water.
(x) Spread the cooled custard over the cake evenly.
(xi) Sprinkle the fruits over it.
(xii) With a knife spread cream over the fruits.
(xiii) Cut cherries to small pieces and sprinkle over pudding and keep the bowl in the fridge to set.

Apple Pie

Preparation Time : 15 minutes **Cooking Time : 30 minutes** **Serves : 4**

Ingredients

Short Crust Pastry

Flour : 175 gms
Amul Butter : 100 gms (from fridge)
Baking Powder : ¼ tsp.
Castor Sugar : 1 tsp.

Filling

Apple : 3 (medium)
Brown Sugar : 4 tbsp.
Cinnamon Powder: ½ tsp.
Nutmeg Powder : ¼ tsp.
Sultanas : 1 tbsp.

Utensil

1 seven inch pie dish

Accompaniment

4 Small Cups Vanilla Ice Cream

Method

(i) Brush the pie dish with butter.
(ii) Prepare crust pastry and divide into 2 parts.
(iii) Sprinkle little maida. Roll out a circle bigger than the circumference of the pie-dish of 1 part of the crust pastry with the help of a rolling pin.
(iv) Place this in the pie dish and spread out evenly and prick with a fork.
(v) Roll out the other half of the crust pastry in the same manner.
(vi) Peel apples and make small pieces and add sultanas, brown sugar, cinnamon powder and nutmeg powder and mix well.
(vii) Add the above mixture in the prepared pie dish.
viii) Place the crust pastry on the filling and cut a plus (+) sign in the centre to release air.
x) Bake in oven at 150°C for 15 to 20 minutes.
xi) When ready, cut the pie in four pieces.
xii) Place one part in serving dish and place ice cream cup on it and serve immediately.

Toffee Top Grape (Cream)

Preparation Time : 5 minutes **Cooking Time : 20 minutes** **Serves : 2**

Ingredients

Seedless Grapes : 500 gms
Fresh Cream : 100 gms
Brown Sugar : 60 gms

Utensils

One deep wide oven-proof dish

Method

(i) Remove the stalks from the grapes and wash them well.
(ii) Beat the cream till thick.
(iii) Place all the grapes at the bottom of the dish and spread cream over it evenly. Keep this in the fridge overnight.
(iv) Pound brown sugar till soft.
(v) Before serving remove the dish from the fridge and sprinkle brown sugar over it evenly.
(vi) Place in the oven at 150°C for 5 minutes. When the sugar begins to melt, serve it.

Apricot Charlotte

Preparation Time : 30 minutes **Cooking Time : 25 minutes** **Serves : 4 to 6**

Ingredients

Apricots : ¼ kg
Bread : 8 slices
Lemon Juice : 1 tbsp.
Lemon Rind : 1 lemon
Amul Butter : 100 gms
Sugar : 1 tbsp.

Utensil

Jelly mould

Method

(i) Soak apricots in water overnight.
(ii) On the following morning, remove seeds and make small pieces.
(iii) Crush the apricots and cook them in water. Add sugar.
(iv) When it cooks add lemon rind and chopped seeds.
(v) Cut out a circle off the bread slice big enough to fit the circular bottom of the jelly mould.
(vi) Cut off the edges of the remaining slices. Cut the bread to strips bigger than ¼" in width.
(vii) Brush the jelly mould with butter.
(viii) Dip all the strips as well as the circular disc (on one side) in melted butter and place strips along the sides and the circular disc in the centre of the mould.
(ix) Add the apricot mixture and sprinkle cut pieces of bread over it. Pour little melted butter over it. Bake in the oven at 150°C till the bread pieces turn golden brown.
(x) Invert on a serving dish.
(xi) Enjoy this dish hot.

Chocolate Coffee Pie

Preparation Time : 15 minutes Cooking Time : 20 minutes **Serves : 4 to 6**

Ingredients

Short Crust Pastry

Flour : 115 gms
Butter : 60 gms

Filling

Milk : 1 Cup
Cornflour : 1 ½ tbsp. full
Cocoa : 1 tsp.
Instant Coffee : 1 tsp.
Butter : 1 tbsp.
Castor Sugar : 3 tbsp.
Fresh Cream : 100 gms
Grated Milk Chocolate : ½ slab

Utensils

6 ½" pipe
Star nozzle
Piping bag

Method

(i) Prepare short crust pastry.
(ii) Roll out a circle bigger, by 1" to 1 ½", than the circumference of the pie-dish. It should be thick.
(iii) Brush the pie-dish with butter and place the circle in the centre of the pie-dish and with a fork, prick it. Pinch the edges of the pastry close to each other. This makes the pie look very attractive and bake.
(iv) Place this pie in the oven at 150°C for 15 to 20 minutes till it turns golden brown.
(v) While the pie is getting ready, prepare the remainder of the recipe mentioned below.
(vi) Prepare a paste by adding coffee, cocoa and cornflour to 2 table spoons milk and mix well.
(vii) To the rest of the milk, add sugar and boil it. When it boils remove from gas and add cocoa mixture and mix well. Place on the gas again and cook for 2 to 3 minutes. Stir continuously. Add butter. Remove from gas and mix well. When it cools, pour into the ready pie-dish and keep in the fridge to set.
(viii) When the pie sets, beat cream till thick.
(ix) Pour the cream in the piping bag fixed with star nozzle and pipe out rosettes along the edge of the pie.
(x) Sprinkle grated chocolate on the rosettes and keep in the fridge.

Apple Mousse

Preparation Time : 15 to 20 minutes Cooking Time : 20 minutes Serves : 6

Ingredients

Apples : 3 large (400-500 gms)
Lemon : 1
Gelatine : 1 level tbsp.
Eggs : 2
Pineapple Essence : ¼ tsp.
Thick Malai from Milk : ½ cup +
Fresh Cream : 1 cup (150 gms)
Castor Sugar : 4 tbsp.

Utensil

Round cake tin : (6 ½" x 1 ¾")

For Decoration

Apple : 1 (small)

Method

(i) Peel and core the apples and cut to small pieces. Apply lemon juice to the pieces.
(ii) Grate lemon peel to form lemon rind and squeeze out juice.
(iii) Add lemon rind and ¼ cup water to the apple pieces and cook till soft and mash it (puree it).
(iv) Mix together 2 table spoons lemon juice and 2 table spoons water and heat it. Add gelatin to it and dissolve it. When it dissolves keep it warm.
(v) Mix the apple pulp and gelatine mixture.
(vi) Beat eggs and sugar by double boiler method (refer method no. : 2) and add essence to it.
(vii) Mix the apple and egg mixture together.
(viii) If using milk and malai, then beat malai with a fork or spoon and add milk to it and mix. Add this to the above mixture and mix well. If using fresh cream then first beat it till thick and add to the above mixture and mix.
(ix) Wet the cake tin.
(x) Transfer the mixture into the cake tin and keep in fridge. It takes 2 hours to set.
(xi) When it sets invert into a plate.
(xii) For decoration, don't peel apples. Just slice them thinly and arrange them on the mousse and chill in the fridge till you serve it. (See page 110 for illustration.)

Important Note : *Depending on the sweetness or sourness of the apples, adjust the amount of sugar accordingly. To make the pudding slide out easily, hold the bottom of the cake tin in the hot water for few seconds. Don't hold it for too long otherwise the pudding will become thin. This dessert tastes better if it is one day old.*

Cabbage Kheer

Preparation Time : 5 minutes Cooking Time : 15 to 20 minutes Serves : 3

Ingredients

Finely Chopped Cabbage : white variety ½ cup (full)
Homemade Ghee : 1 tsp. (thick)
Milk : 1 litre
Sugar : 6 to 8 tsp. or add less or more as per your taste
Nutmeg Powder

Method

(i) Soak grated cabbage in water for 1 hour.
(ii) Wash and drain in a collander.
(iii) Heat ghee in a pan and add cabbage and saute. Cover and cook.
(iv) Add milk and reduce the mixture till it is ¾. Add sugar.
(v) Add nutmeg powder. When it cools, keep in fridge to chill. This has a very different taste more like basundi.

Important Note : *Try and see that the cabbage is whitish in colour so that the kheer stays white.*

Illustration for Punjabi Samosa (see page 82)

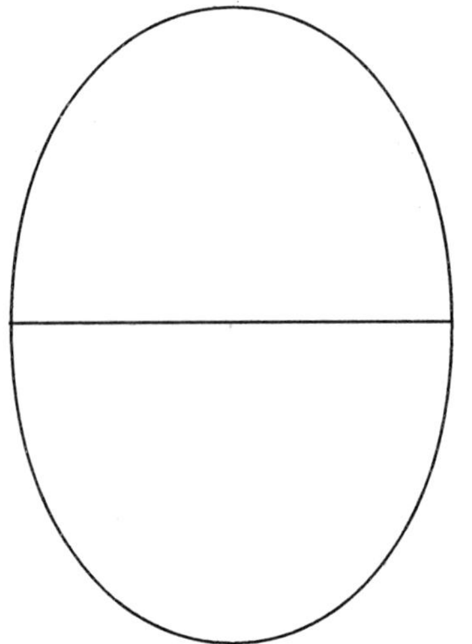

Moisten the portion marked
A, B, C with water

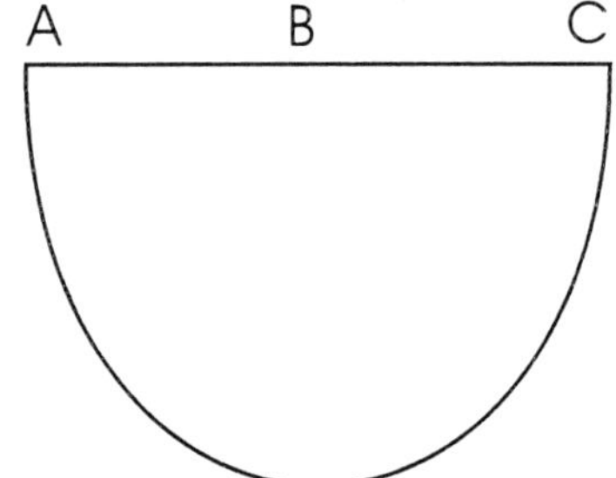

Illustration for Apple Mousse (see page 109)

Glossary

English	Hindi	Marathi
Cucumber	खीरा	काकडी
Knolkhol	गाठगोबी	नवलकोल
Beetroot	चुकंदर	बीट
Potato	आलू	बटाटे
Ginger	अद्रक	आले
Coriander Leaves	हराधनिया	कोथिंबीर
Curry Leaves	मीठा निंब करी पत्ता	कढी लिंब कढी पत्ता
Green Chillies	हरी मिर्च	हिरवी मिरची
Mint Leaves	पुदिना	पुदिना
Green Peas	मटर	मटार
Fenugreek	मेथी	मेथी भाजी
Spinach	पालक	पालक
Ribgourd	तुरीया	शिराळी
Tomato	टमाटर	टोमॅटो
Onion	प्याज	कांदे
Lemon	निंबू	लिंबू
Drumsticks	शींगफली	शेगटाच्या शेंगा
Collocasia	अरबी	अडकुळी
Yam	सुरण, जमीनकंद	सुरण
Capsicum	सिमला मिर्च	बोंगी मिरची
Turnip	सलगम	सलगम
Sultana	खिशमिश	बेदाणा
Almonds	बादाम	बदाम
Pistachio	पिश्ता	पिस्ता
Peanuts	मुंगफली	शेंगदाणे
Raisins	मनुका	मनुका
Dates	खजूर	खजूर
Cashewnuts	काजू	काजू
Charonji	चिरोंजी	चारोळी
Walnuts	आक्रुट	आक्रोड
Papaya	पपीता	पोपया
Apple	सेब	सफरचंद
Custard Apple	सीताफल	सीताफळ
Grapes	अंगूर	द्राक्षे
Sweet Lime	मोसंबी	मोसंबी
Orange	नारंगी	संत्री
Banana	केला	केळी

English	Hindi	Marathi
Mango	आम	आंबा
Watermelon	कलिंगर	कलिंगड
Cantaloups	खरबूज	खरबूज
Pineapple	अननस	अननस
Grapefruit	पपनस	पपनस
Figs	अंजीर	अंजीर
Guava	अमृद	पेरू
Rice	चावल	तांदूळ
Toor Dal	तूअर डाल	तुरीची डाळ
Lentil	काला मसूर	मसूर
Split Black Beans	उरदकी डाल	उडदाची डाळ
Split Green Beans	मुंग डाल	मूगाची डाळ
Whole Green Beans	मूग साबूत	मूग
Whole Black Beans	उडद साबूत	उडीद
Gram	चना	हरभरा
Flour	मैदा	मैदा
White Kidney Beans	चौली	चवळी
Red Kidney Beans	राजमा	राजमा
Red Chilli	लाल मिर्च	लाल मिरची
Turmeric Powder	हलदी	हळद
Salt	नमक	मीठ
Black Pepper	काली मिर्च	काळी मिरी
Whole Coriander	सुखा धनिया	धने
Cumin Seeds	जिरा	जिरे
Black Cumin	काला जिरा	शहाजिरे
Cinnamon	तज	दालचिनी
Cloves	लौंग	लवंग
Green Cardamom	इलायची	वेलघी
Black Cardamom	बडी इलायची	मोठी वेलची
Fennel Seeds	सौंफ	बडिशेप
Asafoetida	हिंग	हिंग
Mustard	राई	मोहरी
Bay Leaf	तेजपत्ता	तमालपत्र
Poppy Seeds	खशखश	खसखस
Sesame Seeds	तील	तीळ
Pomegranate Seeds	अनारदाना	डाळिंबाचे दाणे

English	Hindi	Marathi
Tamarind	इमली	चिंच
Saffron	केसर, जाफ्रान	केशर
Coconut	नारियल	नारळ
Dry Coconut	नारियलका बुरदा	सुके खोबरे
Nutmeg	जायफल	जायफळ
Mace	जावत्री	जायपत्री
Carom Seeds or Thymol Seeds	अजवान	ओवा
Dry Ginger	सोंठ	सुंठ
Kokum	कुकम	आमसूल
Amchur	आमचूर	आमचूर
Spices	मसाला	मसाला
Nigella	कलोंजी	कांद्याचे बी
Jaggery	गूर	गूळ
Garlic	लस्सन	लसूण
Black Salt	काला नमक	सैधंव
Vinegar	सिरका	आंब
Basil leaves	तुलसी	तुळस मंजिरी
Carrot	गाजर	गाजर

English	Hindi	Marathi
Lady's Finger	भिंडी	भेंडे
Pumpkin	कद्दु	लाल भोपळा
Bottlegourd	दुधी, लौकी	दुधी भोपळा
Cauliflower	फुलगोभी	फ्लॉवर
Cabbage	बंध गोभी	कोबी
Snake Gourd	पडबल	पडवळ
Brinjal	बैंगन	वांगी
Egg Plant	बैंगन	बाण वांगे
White Pumpkin	पेठा	कोहळा
Sweet Potato	शकरकंदी	रताळी
Jack Fruit	कटहल	फणस
String Beans	लोभिया	चवळी शेंगा
French Beans	फ्रासबीन	फरसबी
Bittergourd	करेला	कारली
Curd Cheese	छाना	चक्का
Cottage Cheese	पनीर/छाना	पनीर
Oil added for crispness	मोहन	मोहन
Clarified Butter	घी	घी

कृतींची शब्दसूची

English	Hindi	Marathi
to grind	पिसना	वाटणे
to saute	भूनना	परतणे
to cook	पकाना	शिजवणे
to boil	उबालना	उकळणे
to parboil	आध पक्का उबालना	अर्धवट उकडणे
to fry	तलना	तळणे
shallow fry	कम तेल मे तलना	तव्यावर तेल घालून बदामी करणे
to marinate	मसाला लगाकर रखना	मसाला लावून ठेवणे
to cut fine	महीन काटना	बारीक चिरणे
to grate	कदु कस करना	किसणे
to beat	फेटना	फेटणे
to stir	हिलाना	ढवळणे
to prove	खमीर उठ आना	फुगण्यास ठेवणे
Temper	तडका/छोक	फोडणी/फोडणी देणे
to sprinkle	भुरकाना	पेरणे

English	Hindi	Marathi
grind to paste	बारीक पिसना	गंध वाटणे
to mash	नरम करना	मऊ करणे
to peel	छिलका उतारना	साल काढणे
to roll	बेलना	लाटणे
to turn upside down	पलटना	उलटणे
to knead	मलना	मळणे
to strain	छानना	गाळणे
to dice	टुकडा काटना	तुकडे करणे
to mix	एकठ्ठा करना	एकत्र करणे
to blanch	उबालके ठंडे पानी में डालना	थोडेस उकळून थंड पाण्यात टाकणे
to puree	पीसना	बलक करणे
to steam	उबालना	उकडणे
to slice	पतला काटना	काप काढणे
to churn	मदानी करना	घुसळणे